Kudos for *Stop the Vanilla*

"Steve's Stop the Vanilla processes were a game changer for our organization, our team members, and me. With the help of Stop the Vanilla, LLC we have created a culture of growth and opportunity that is centered around understanding each individual's gifts, passions, and overall life goals. By staying focused on developing the total person and fostering an environment where everyone should love to come to work, we have achieved consistent 20 percent year-over-year growth and a 98 percent retention rate. And along the way I also found that leading the organization in the role of Shepherd of the Talent is my true calling."

–Terry Albrecht
President/Owner Packer Fastener/Coach to every team member.

"This book is a must-read for anyone who aspires to become the best version of themselves. The vision that all high school students have a customized career plan by the time they graduate is closer to reality."

–Damian LaCroix
Superintendent, Howard-Suamico School District
2017 Wisconsin Superintendent of the Year

"Career and life planning are an essential part of total player development, and this process will ensure we deliver that for every student athlete."

—Bryce Paup
Assistant Football Coach, University of Northern Iowa
1995 NFL Defensive Player of the Year

"This is the first career planning book that I've seen that uses behavioral science to reveal a career fit just for you. It has become a required read for all of my students."

—Eliot Elfner
Emeritus Professor of Business Administration,
St. Norbert College

"We all deserve lives we love. Through a step-by-step process that is based on decades of experience and research on human behavior, Steve Van Remortel shares a simple but profound career and life-planning process to uncover your passions. Steve has a gift for helping people step into their true calling and reach meaningful success. Just like he has transformed the lives of so many clients and colleagues, *Stop the Vanilla in Your Career & Life* will help you find passion and purpose in your work— and in your life."

—Stacy Ennis
Speaker, trainer, bestselling coauthor of *Growing Influence: A Story of How to Lead with Character, Expertise, and Impact*

"The simple, four-step process Steve shares is practical and proven to work based on the countless stories of people and leaders he's helped. This book will assist you in writing a new story for your career and life—one of passion and meaning. Read this book if you want more out of your career and life."

—Paul Smith
Three-time best-selling author including,
The 10 Stories Great Leaders Tell

STOP THE
VANILLA
IN YOUR CAREER
AND LIFE

PLATFORM
PUBLISHING

For ordering books, special discounts, bulk purchases, or information about our products or services, please visit our website at www.stopthevanilla.com, or contact the author at info@stopthevanilla.com

Softcover book, eBook, and audio book of *Stop the Vanilla in Your Career and Life* are distributed by Platform Publishing.

Library of Congress Control Number: 2020917099

Library of Congress Cataloging-in-Publication Data is on file with the publisher.

Publishers Cataloging-in-Publication Data

Stop the Vanilla in Your Career and Life.; by Steve Van Remortel

160 pages cm.

ISBNs: 978-1-7357303-0-1 Paperback
978-1-7357303-2-5 ePub
978-1-7357303-3-2 Mobi
978-1-7357303-1-8 Audiobook

Printed in the United States of America

Contents

Foreword | v

Introduction | ix

1: Let's Talk About Vanilla. 1

2: Your Mint Chocolate Chip 14

3: Own the Cone 31

4: Sweet Options. 58

5: Your Rocky Road Life Map 94

6: Fire Up the Ice Cream Truck .113

7: The Next Scoop 124

8: Just Desserts. 132

Summary of Steps To Develop Your Career and Life Plan | 138

Acknowledgements | 140

About the Author | 145

iii

This book is dedicated to the 87.7 percent
of the working population that does not
describe themselves as passionate about what
they do for a living.

*It is time for you to love what you do
to live the life you want.*

Foreword

The majority of working Americans—an estimated 87 percent[1]—lack excitement and passion for their work. This has grave consequences, not just to their work, but to their lives and to those closest to them.

> Steve Van Remortel says, "When you aren't passionate about your work, you're more likely to stress-eat, exercise less, suffer from illness and disease, feel depressed or anxious, abuse alcohol, lose sleep, feel irritable and fatigued, and lose all sense of motivation."

I know this firsthand. Not that long ago, I was among this majority. But that's not where my story ends, and that's not where yours has to end either.

---

1. John Hagel III et al., *Passion at Work: Cultivating Worker Passion as a Cornerstone of Talent Development*, Passion at work - Deloitte (Deloitte University Press, 2014), https://www2.deloitte.com/us/en/insights/topics/talent/worker-passion-employee-behavior.html.

Steve Van Remortel also says "…when you love the work you do, it hardly feels like work at all. You have more energy, show more enthusiasm, feel a deeper capacity to help others, eat better, exercise more, and have more motivation than ever before. Pursuing your passion. . . will absolutely energize you. . . ."

If you are willing to put in the work, be honest with yourself, and be persistent in the process, the principles in this book will help you wrap your natural behavioral style around a passion in your life. It will bring about more energy and productive output than you ever thought possible, as it did for me.

What follows in this book is a simple but powerful analogy. Work devoid of passion is like vanilla ice cream—a universal default flavor that is at best a base for other toppings or a supplement to other desserts. On the other hand, work built on passion is like refreshing, sweet, unique, and colorful mint chocolate chip ice cream. And work built on passion that is also in line with your natural behavior style—that is like mint chocolate ice cream in a solid cone, ready to be enjoyed on a hot summer day.

Each chapter covers a different aspect of this analogy—from considering the drawbacks of vanilla in your career and finding your own Mint Chocolate Chip, to "owning your cone" and creating your "Rocky Road Life Map."

In building out this analogy, Steve Van Remortel draws on decades of experience as a business leader and executive coach. Steve was actually my third executive coach at a low point in my career. A mentor of mine took the DISC behavioral assessment tool Steve describes and found it to be spot-on accurate for him. He recommended that it would be helpful for me too. Indeed, it was.

Steve is masterful at drawing out passions in a way that compliments your natural behavioral style. I experienced this firsthand. In one of our coaching sessions, we were discussing a particular company and position I was pursuing. Steve sensed a disconnect, and he relentlessly probed my motivations and passion regarding this company and position. Then Steve drew together several distinct threads from previous coaching sessions and asked me about my excitement regarding those threads.

I'll never forget Steve's reaction to my response: He slammed his pen on the table and slid it and a piece of paper in my direction. "Articulate that level of passion in an interview," Steve said, "and you'll have an offer on the spot!" As my passion further evolved, it became clear that it would not be realized in the context of another gig in corporate America, but rather through a firm of my own—one that I started within two months of that coaching session.

Since that point, my journey has not been without bumps and setbacks that Steve talks about in the chapter called, "Your Rocky Road Life Map." But the journey only began when I stopped being satisfied with vanilla and started pursuing *my* Mint Chocolate Chip in *my* cone. And having now tasted it, I won't ever go back. My firm is growing, and I am truly passionate about helping clients who are on the front lines of medical and technical innovation.

I have moved from the 87 percent of working Americans who lack excitement and passion in their work, to the coveted 13 percent who are passionate about their work. And you can do this too! But your journey won't begin until you stop being satisfied with vanilla and take the time to find *your* Mint Chocolate Chip and own *your* cone.

I encourage you to enjoy the journey through the pages of this book.

Bon appetite,

—Matthew J. Smyth
President & Chief Strategist,
Headland Law & Strategy

Introduction

Welcome to the first day of the rest of your life.

When you look back on this day, you will realize it was the start of something great. It was the beginning of your journey towards loving what you do for a living to live the life you want.

That day for me happened over twenty years ago. It was the day I took my first behavioral science assessment. It showed me the objective strengths of my natural wiring and how they relate to my passions. It allowed me to see how I would use those strengths to love what I do, deliver it naturally, excel at it and get rewarded for it.

As I experienced a more meaningful and blessed life from having a career at the intersection of my passions and strengths, I wanted to provide the same experience for my children. As you may have experienced, very few of us leave high school with answers to the tough questions: What am I passionate about? What am I naturally good at? What is the best career path for me?

As I helped each of my four children define a career path that they would love, I created and fine-tuned this simple, four-step career and life planning process. At that moment, it did not cross my mind to share this process with others.

It was not until I discovered through working with countless leadership teams that two or three members of each team were not passionate about their work. This didn't happen just once in a while. This happened hundreds of times.

Something needed to be done, so I dusted off the career and life planning process and have shared it with countless individuals who now love what they do for a living. And that journey starts here for you.

Before you continue reading I encourage you to join our private Facebook Group to work through your challenges along the way. In the group, you will be able to engage with, learn, and gain support from others making the same life-changing transformation. You can join by going to Facebook.com/groups/stvcareerandlife. I look forward to hearing your success story!

When people ask you how you became passionate about your career and intentional about living a meaningful life, you will point back to today as being the first day of the rest of your life. It's time to Stop the Vanilla in Your Career and Life!

Let's Talk About Vanilla

As nice as a scoop of ice cream can be, no one ever screams for vanilla—not with all the other exciting flavors available. Vanilla ice cream is okay when it's a blank canvas to be decorated with our choice of caramel, hot fudge, chocolate chips, cookie dough, or rainbow sprinkles. Vanilla ice cream goes well with a sweet slice of apple pie. But vanilla on its own? Not so much. As a matter of fact, vanilla is such a notoriously dull flavor that the word has become shorthand for anything bland, basic, common, or neutral. Vanilla is the universal default flavor.

If plain vanilla is your only choice, well, it is better than nothing, but plenty of other options exist. Besides, better than nothing is not your style! If it were, there is no way you would be reading this book. While most of you would never order a plain vanilla dessert, you may be settling for plain vanilla in your career, and by extension, in your life as well.

Take someone who loves spending time outdoors and consider how they'd feel spending forty hours a week behind a desk, under fluorescent lights. Or, take someone who lives on the energy they get from social interaction and consider how they'd do spending Monday through Friday with nothing but silence or music in their ears. If you're currently at a job where you *can* work instead of where you *want* to work, you're hardly alone. Only 12.3 percent of America's workforce describe themselves as passionate about their work, according to a 2014 survey reported by Deloitte[1]. That's less than 13 percent! It sure lends new emphasis to the term *workforce*, doesn't it?

Only 12.3 percent of America's workforce describe themselves as passionate about their work.

Let's raise that percentage, starting with you! As you'll soon learn, you already have what you need to make it happen. Stop robotically slapping that snooze button on weekday mornings. It's time to put an end to feeling so drained by Friday that you can't enjoy your weekend, get caught up on housework, or recharge your battery before snoozing the Monday morning alarm all over again. Cut the talk of long hours and the lack of satisfaction from your conversations. Instead, whet your appetite for a more satisfying scenario: finishing each day eager to begin the next.

Weeks don't need to turn into years, nor do your professional or personal relationships need to be impacted by

1. ibid.

stress. Most of all, you don't need to neglect yourself, or suppress your dreams, desires, and ambitions. Can you imagine if instead of pursuing an acting career, Harrison Ford had kept working as a carpenter? What if Ellen DeGeneres had stuck to shucking oysters, or Whoopi Goldberg had remained a morgue beautician? With respect to Whoopi's clientele, those entertainers escaped some dead-end jobs! The longer you wait, the more you are missing out on.

At this very minute, you are capable of starting an upward spiral of momentum in your life. Together we can kick our commonplace, colorless, and claustrophobic careers to the curb. Regardless of the time, energy, or resources you've invested in this path that's turned out more treadmill than yellow brick road, it is never too late to make a positive change. Beware: Out of desperation for change, some people jump from one job they hate to another job that is not a good fit either. The process detailed in this book will ensure you make purpose-driven, true-to-you career moves and life decisions.

You already have within you the two ingredients needed to stop living vanilla: a *passion* in your life and a fixed, natural *behavioral style*. You might not be able to iden-

Merriam-Webster Dictionary defines passion as: "A strong liking or desire for or devotion to some activity, object, or concept."

tify each of these things immediately, but you will soon! Our passions are the things we are enthusiastic about, that spark our imagination, and preoccupy our thoughts. Our natural behavior style is hardwired in each of us. It's about how we communicate and interact with others and the world. When we uncover our natural behavior style and wrap it around our passion, we can live a life more fulfilling than we ever thought possible. It's a recipe for sweet success!

Living a Passion, Not Just Having a Job

Consider the middle-aged manager who has chosen job security and the familiarity of routine over personal satisfaction and career growth. Consider the fifty-five-year-old professional squeezed out and displaced all in the name of corporate downsizing. Consider the employee who, in spite of being known for having company loyalty, seems to be holding back. Increasingly disengaged, that employee is both unable to contribute effectively, and unaware of his or her unique strengths. Consider the empty-nester who's spent the last twenty-five years raising children, managing household finances, and juggling schedules, who can't imagine how to reenter an evolved workforce. Consider the recent high school or college graduate who has long-term career aspirations. Whether it be dreams of becoming a novelist, electrician, salesperson, congressman, or director of a nonprofit, the graduate can't find that first stepping-stone and begins to question if their dream can be achieved. We've all seen lack of direction and uncertainty dominate the high school or college senior.

Those who aren't excited by their work are plagued with a constant drone of anxiety, and if that's worn off, they feel numb. I don't have to tell you that this affects their whole life. This affliction affects everyone, from those working a placeholder job just to pay rent, to those who are solidly employed (and perhaps well paid), yet not passionate about their work. The latter individual may appear to the outsider to be all set and secure, even happy. Internally, he or she craves a genuinely fulfilling career. The pressure to gut it out for that next paycheck is real. When weighing the risks and rewards of change against the responsibilities of mortgage payments, paying for daycare or children's activities, or finding time to help aging parents, making a big change is downright scary. Health insurance alone can scare even the most ingenious entrepreneurs into surrendering to a vanilla job, even when they admit that real success and happiness are at stake. Uncertainty and insecurity lock out otherwise ambitious people from pursuing their passions.

This stressful inner conflict, as well as the energy sapped from adapting to a poor-fitting job, will eventually exhaust even the best of us. If you're not fulfilled by your work, what may start as a decent gig with adequate pay, it can rapidly devolve into a job that takes more from you than it provides. Whether you're still in high school or recently retired—without direction and a sense of passion you will feel unfulfilled—guaranteed.

Pursuing your passion, on the other hand, will absolutely energize you. I'm talking about rejuvenation with a capital R. The zeal for doing what you love is invigorating—like a battery that recharges itself. We all know someone who is passionate about their work, and the temptation is to think they were just born with enthusiasm, or they were just lucky they found their thing so easily. When you firmly believe in your career path, you'll take pride in even the most repetitive tasks, while finding the new or unexpected challenges exciting. There isn't an absence of hard work, it's just that hard work feels satisfying and worthwhile.

The most important move of my career was neither moving to a bigger city nor changing jobs. It was making my passion my priority. Doing so is the primary reason I can count myself among that coveted 12.3 percent. My only frustration is that I hadn't adopted this mindset sooner. I'll share more later, but for now, let's just say that my path was far from smooth. I went from aimless as a teenager, to restless in my twenties, to jobless in my thirties. I especially wish I could have assured my thirty-five-year-old self—a father of four who was suddenly and unexpectedly unemployed—that he was finally embarking on a path to personal freedom. I had experienced a vanilla life for too long. Since then, I've been on a journey that is anything but vanilla! I found my natural behavioral style and my passion, and most importantly, how to love what I do by combining them.

I have created a process to help others avoid the slumps, scares, rejection, and unfulfilled ambition that comes from living a life without passion. I've crafted this process of personal transformation during the twenty-plus years I've spent following my own passion—which I boil down to one word: strategy. I'm passionate about creating strategies that will accomplish ambitious goals. That's why I founded Stop The Vanilla, LLC. As chief strategist and talent advisor, I've worked with thousands of companies and found that virtually all of them have employees whose position is a poor fit for their natural behavioral style. For example, having an introverted person making sales calls, or an extroverted person working by themselves all day. Unless we understand ourselves, we don't know which direction we should go in these big decisions.

Still, these employees trudge onward, from 8 a.m. to 5 p.m. or longer. Working harder and longer gets the job done, but does not ignite their fervor. Their paychecks could keep the lights on at home, but money alone isn't brightening their outlook on life. Some have pursued a path that is not meeting their needs, while others had external forces push them into a field they were not passionate about. They were dissatisfied citizens of "Vanilla-Ville."

Just like you, they have passions and a natural behavioral style, and they have what it takes to stop the vanilla in their career and life. Perhaps like too many of us, they hadn't clarified their passions, and spent too many years putting their job before themselves. Or maybe they didn't know or understand their natural behavioral style and how it affected them, their career, and their relationships. What a thrill it is to see this lightbulb finally come on for people! My passion for strategy and behavioral science, and my action-oriented behavioral style have led me to help so many through this unique process of clarification—guiding them to love what they do and live the life they want.

Now it's your turn. I've written this book to help you begin to understand the crucial aspects of your behavioral style and unique skill set, and to successfully apply them to a joyful and important career—in such a way that you'll never have a "job" again.

As you go through this transformational process, have confidence in the Stop the Vanilla in Your Career and Life Process because it is based on countless hours of hands-on research and experience coaching thousands of individuals. Give yourself permission to dream about the day you'll look forward to Mondays. Conjure up your fantasy of going after what you want with gusto. Imagine being paid to do something you love!

Are you ready to see what that looks like for you? What that *feels* like for you? I can tell you from experience, the feeling goes far beyond the financial reward.

Self-Actualization

It takes just one bad day at work to know your career and life are inextricably linked—one affects the other. Working forty-plus hours a week at a job you aren't passionate about means less time to spend on your family relationships, social life, hobbies, self-care, and creative outlets. When you aren't passionate about your work, you're more likely to stress-eat, exercise less, suffer from illness and disease, feel depressed or anxious, abuse alcohol, lose sleep, feel irritable and fatigued, and lose all sense of motivation. Our career choices are nothing short of essential.

Conversely, when you love the work you do, it hardly feels like work at all. You have more energy, show more enthusiasm, feel a deeper capacity to help others, eat better, exercise more, and have more motivation than ever before. This book will help you put an end to vanilla in your career—thereby improving your personal life too. With the clarity this four-step process provides, you'll gain focus and infuse a sense of purpose into virtually every move you make.

The Stop the Vanilla in Your Career and Life Process is pragmatic and based on scientifically measurable traits of human behavior. But at the heart of it is your pursuit of true satisfaction. This yearning isn't frivolous, or a sign of greed. It is a human *need* called self-actualization. Fortunately, in Western society our basic physiological needs—food, water, and shelter—are met for most of us. Anyone born in a first-world country inherits this incredible head start toward self-actualization—the pinnacle of human needs according to famous psychologist Abraham Maslow's Hierarchy of Needs.

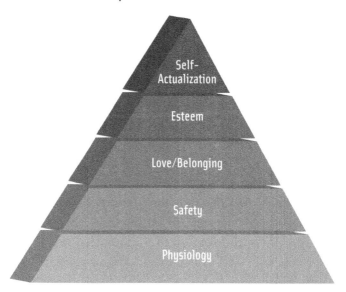

Beyond the requirements for survival, Maslow places self-actualization as the maximization of our potential, the full expression of our talents, the fulfillment of our aspirations. This is why a person could have so much going for them—safety, love, financial security—and still feel unfulfilled. "What a man can be, he must be," Maslow asserted.

Still, self-actualization is rarely discussed in career and life planning. The people in that passionate 12.3 percent, though, have either attained self-actualization, or are rapidly approaching it—enjoying the wave of momentum they've created for themselves along the way.

How did the 12.3 percent get there? It wasn't just blind luck or even raw ambition. Individuals who have attained self-actualization are as diverse as the very passions they've pursued, but one trait they've all had in common is the will to transcend a vanilla existence.

The Four-Step Process

A fortunate minority of employees love the work they do to earn a living, but every single one of us, from any background whatsoever (race, gender, ethnicity), can achieve his or her dream. People have gone professional in every arena—art, business, counseling, sports, construction, science, entrepreneurship, education, government, you name it—thanks to their commitment to blowing past the bland. Some make it seem like they were born with a plan, but that was definitely not me. For far too long, I hardly even knew how off-track I was, and yet I stumbled my way to clarity. I not only want to help you live the life you've always wanted, but I also want you to get there a lot faster than I did. This is something of a family recipe, by the way. My kids have been following it since they were teenagers, with results beyond what I could have imagined. I'll be sure to share some of those stories with you later on.

There are four steps to this career and life planning process; each will be explored more fully in the chapters that follow.

Step 1: Define Your Mint Chocolate Chip

If vanilla is plain, mint chocolate chip is passion. It's refreshing, sweet, unique, and colorful. Step 1 will walk you through a thoughtful process to define your passions. This can be a powerful time of discovery!

Step 2: Own Your Cone

Like mint chocolate chip ice cream on a hot summer day, passion can melt away if not enjoyed in a timely fashion. An ice cream cone, however, is solid and consistent, just like your natural behavioral style. This process is unique, and works because we use an online behavioral science assessment that measures four different traits: Dominance, Influence, Steadiness, and Compliance. This instrument is widely used by companies to screen potential employees and develop current ones into leaders. It is best used to learn more about yourself and your colleagues, so you can communicate and collaborate more effectively. In Step 2, you will learn how to understand, own, and ultimately leverage your unique, natural behavioral style for your eternal benefit.

Step 3: Explore Your Sweet Options

After defining your passion(s) and natural behavioral style, the third step will be to taste-test your favorite flavors. Multiple careers can fit successfully with different combinations of passions and styles. An array of examples here will help you work through and select your Mint Chocolate Chip Strategy—the customized career plan that wraps your natural style around a passion in your life. Step 3 will help you explore options for your strategy and discover tips for determining which opportunities will lead to the life you want.

Step 4: Create Your Rocky Road Life Map

The road of life can no doubt get rocky, but that is why a map is so important. Bumps that could otherwise throw you off-course won't deter you from your destination with a life map. In Step 4, you will define your legacy, your long-term objectives, and short-term action plans to make your Mint Chocolate Chip a reality and live the life you want.

As you complete this process, you will recognize: "Without passion, your natural style is not focused; without understanding your natural style, your passion is not enjoyed." This process will lead to the life you want through a personal strategy and talent plan.

Not unlike the airline instruction of securing your own oxygen mask before helping those around you, first you've got to ensure *you* are personally living a passionate life and shepherding your own talents before you can show others how. Using real-life examples (including my own blunders and breakthroughs), this book will lead you through a journey of illumination and self-improvement to start loving what you do for a living to live the life you want.

The Scoop on Next Steps

Options for you to complete the process as you go through the book are as follows:

- Download the PDFs of the Passions Worksheet, the Mint Chocolate Chip Strategy and the Rocky Road Life Map templates at StopTheVanilla.com/ Resources.

- Subscribe to the Stop the Vanilla Career and Life Planning Course at Courses.StopTheVanilla.com.

2

Your Mint Chocolate Chip

"The only way to do great work is to love what you do. If you haven't found it yet, keep looking. Don't settle. As with all matters of the heart, you'll know when you find it."

— Steve Jobs

From college dropout to CEO of Apple Inc., Steve Jobs exemplified how you can be obsessed with your passion and get rewarded for it. His advice to have the courage to follow your heart was delivered in his commencement address at Stanford University in June 2005, about a year after he was diagnosed with pancreatic cancer. With keen awareness of the limits of time, he suggested that you "Don't waste it living someone else's life." Jobs, one of history's wealthiest innovators, believed his success was a direct result of his commitment to always pursue his passion.

We all like to do what we are good at. The more we do the things we like, the better we will get and the more we'll like doing them. It's a self-perpetuating phenomenon—an upward spiral.

"At its most basic level, it's just about you...It's really about your personal interests," said Ben Silbermann in a 2019 CNN Business interview when asked about an app he had developed. Silbermann has come a long way from a kid who collected bugs growing up in Des Moines, Iowa, yet he has always maintained his passion for collecting. "Collecting tells a lot about who you are," Silbermann mused at a 2013 conference. But did he *always* know who he was?

Silbermann wound up majoring in political science in college, but like many millennials, the degree he earned would not directly figure into his future career. After graduating, he spent several years working as a consultant before Google hired him in 2006 to run advertising. It was a great job for someone in his late 20s, to be sure, but still not Silbermann's dream job. Throughout it all, he never lost his belief in the concept of cultivating and expressing one's identity via the collection of tangible objects, which was at odds with his digital career. But what if he could combine his lifelong passion with his recently acquired professional experience?

Inspired by Google's own modest-to-meteoric rise to the top of the tech world, Silbermann recruited a college buddy and a mutual friend to start developing an online platform—something that could serve as a virtual bulletin board, where users could curate collections and share their ideas, and by extension—their personalities. They began working on their start-up in their spare time, and after just a few false starts creating various iPhone apps, Silbermann and his collaborators finally perfected their platform in 2010. Silbermann was able to leave Google to run the app—which they had named Pinterest—full time. Pinterest's popularity has since expanded to attract about a quarter-billion users every month, with a value of roughly $11 billion. Inspiring creativity in people worldwide—not bad for a bug collector!

Ken Jeong is another example of someone whose work may have added enjoyment to your life, even if you don't know his name. He was born in 1969 to South Korean immigrants in Detroit and raised in North Carolina, where he graduated from high school at age sixteen. Jeong graduated from Duke University, and by age twenty-six, he had finished medical school and relocated to New Orleans to complete his residency. For someone so academically successful, you would guess Jeong's passion to have been medicine. But after he left the hospital, when many doctors might golf away their stress, he would unwind from his ultra-serious day job by performing stand-up and improvisational comedy.

While maintaining employment as a doctor, Jeong developed something of a comedic alter ego, excelling at his atypical hobby and even winning a prominent stand-up comedy competition. The prize: a chance to perform at the Hollywood Improv in Los Angeles. That experience was so positive, it prompted Jeong and his wife to move to L.A., where he continued to work as a licensed physician. After signing with an agent and auditioning for various movie roles, the opportunities trickled in and eventually grew bigger. His patients at the hospital began to recognize him from his appearances. Today, many people recognize Jeong from his breakout role as Mr. Chow in *The Hangover* trilogy and many other feature films and television roles. Jeong earns far more than he would have as a doctor and gets more time off—and he has done so by living a passion, not just having a job. In so many ways, it pays to Stop the Vanilla in Your Career and Life!

Debra Jane Sivyer grew up with a passion for cookies. She was one of five children raised in working-class Oakland by a mother who approached cooking like any other routine household chore—expend minimal effort, get it done, and move on to what is next. Sivyer, hungry as she may have been, never enjoyed her mother's bland, uninspired meals, except the cookies they frequently had for dessert. She even began baking her own cookies, using the inexpensive, imitation ingredients her family could afford. At age thirteen, when Sivyer got her first job, she spent her first paycheck on real butter and chocolate for her next batch of cookies. Without knowing, she was devoting her time and limited resources to feed her passion—that would eventually lead to an incredible career.

After a stint at junior college, Sivyer married an investment banker named Randy Fields. Even though she was happy, she felt the need to do more. Her father had always told her real wealth comes from doing what you love…and what she loved was baking cookies. So, she did. A *lot*. Today, as founder of Mrs. Fields Bakeries, Debra Fields is worth tens of millions of dollars!

Jim Koch also had a recipe to share with the world—at least with those of drinking age. In 1984, Koch was making good money working as a manufacturing consultant in Boston when he happened to unearth his great-great-grandfather's recipe for lager from his dad's attic. Trying out the recipe in his kitchen, Koch discovered he thoroughly enjoyed the process of brewing beer. Though it was new to him, his Austrian ancestors had brewed beer for generations. In fact, Koch believed so strongly in the potential of his family's recipe, that he co-founded a brewery, investing $100,000 of his own money to do so.

Had he sampled too much of his own lager? Though it may have seemed reckless to some, Koch abandoned his reliable and prosperous consulting career to fully pursue his passion, and it paid off. Naming his first product after a famous Bostonian who had also inherited the tradition of brewing, the Samuel Adams Boston Lager won awards in its first year. Today, roughly four million barrels of Koch's great-great-grandfather's beer are brewed annually by his Boston Beer Company, which is now the largest American-owned brewery, currently brewing over seventy styles of Sam Adams beer, cider, and more.

Some of us share passions with ancestors or with siblings, as was the case with Danielle and Jodie Snyder. As early as ages nine and twelve respectively, the two sisters bonded over a desire to create jewelry together, taking their father's medical tools and making earrings and necklaces. After Jodie was hired at a local high-end jewelry store, she bravely asked her boss if their creations could be displayed and sold there. Her boss agreed, and the jewelry was a local sensation. While working together, chasing their unlikely dream, and gaining college and real-world experience, they also earned their brand, Dannijo, a vast success, with famous fans such as Natalie Portman, Rhianna, and Kim Kardashian.

There is a common thread to these diverse stories of success. If settling for the safety of the status quo is living vanilla, then these individuals made the bold move to instead pursue their passions. I call such a passion your Mint Chocolate Chip—chosen for its classic combination of refreshing mint and sweet chocolate because they represent both the satisfaction and the excitement you experience when pursuing your passion. Feel free to substitute the name of your favorite flavor of ice cream in its place!

Favorite Flavors

Social networking, comedy, cookies, beer, and jewelry may work for others, but what is *your* Mint Chocolate Chip? Below is an example of my Passions Worksheet.

Rank	Steve's Passions Worksheet	★
	Hockey	
	Strategy	
	Differentiation	
	Planning	
	Developing Talent in Others	
	Helping Others Achieve Their Goals	
	Healthy Lifestyle/Working Out	

Even if you're already certain of what your passions are, jot down as many as you can in the middle column in the worksheet below. There are no wrong answers here. Simply write whatever comes to mind, even if it's one single passion. Ignore the first and third columns for now. I will help you add to the list afterward.

Rank	Your Passions Worksheet	★

While I hope you enjoyed thinking about some of your favorite things in life, I have worked with enough people—from teenagers to retirees—to know such a list isn't easy for everyone to complete. In some cases, a passion may be so obvious and feature so prominently in your life that you take it for granted and don't recognize it as a passion at all. For others, especially with smart phones, a state of near-constant stimulation and social connection means fewer moments of personal reflection, and greater difficulty recognizing one's individuality. Some have a hard time knowing which interests are their own and not those of their peers or the byproduct of a popular trend.

Unique Strengths and Weaknesses

Natural or exceptional talent can drive a person's passion. We all like to do things we are good at, but what if we don't know what we're good at? At the risk of sounding judgmental, modern practices of sheltering our youth from constructive criticism and true competition (i.e. participation trophies for all) have deprived them of first-hand knowledge of what they do exceptionally well, a valuable indicator for identifying one's passions. Further, social pressures to fit in and conform can discourage idiosyncrasies, which may symbolize someone's unique strengths instead of weaknesses. Ask yourself: What is something you like that no one else seems to be interested in? Personality quirks or eccentricities often reveal your passions.

Whether you couldn't come up with a single passion for your Passions Worksheet, or you needed a second page to contain them all, the following questions will help you brainstorm and discover passions to add to your worksheet:

- What do you love to do?

- What are your hobbies?

- What do you collect?

- What subject or activity gives you energy?

- What can grab your attention so tightly that you will forget to eat?

- What were the classes in high school or college that you were really good at?

- What gets you up early and keeps you up late?

- What have you always had a knack for? What seems to come easier to you than to other people?

- What type of shows, movies, books, magazines, or podcasts do you enjoy? Which websites do you visit regularly?

- If you were paid to write a book on the topic of your choice, what would it be about?

- If you suddenly had an open hour, how would you spend it?

- Which topics do you find yourself searching for on Google? Is there a common theme?

- If you knew you could not fail at something, what would you want to try?

- If money were no object, what would you do?

Perhaps give yourself a day or two to see what you can think of, or even show it to someone who knows you well to see if they can add insight. Remember, it's *your* worksheet, and it is a living, limitless document.

Now look back at the passions you have listed. How do you feel when you focus on what you want and like? In a word, I hope it makes you feel *alive*. Your soul needs sustenance, and while it won't starve on a diet of vanilla, it much prefers mint chocolate chip.

Picking the Cream of the Crop

Your next step in gaining clarity and deciding where to apply your time, energy, and talents is to rank the passions in column one in your worksheet. In your Passions Worksheet, enter "1" beside what you consider to be your greatest passion, "2" beside your second-most, and so on. You are not eliminating any options here, simply focusing more intently on what will get you jacked up about life. (You will find out what to do with the third column of the worksheet in the next section.)

If only 12.3 percent of the workforce describes themselves as passionate about their career, did the rest ever take the time to write down what their passions actually are? An inordinate amount of young people developed a "passion" for achieving good grades. It's not a bad goal, but what about the next seventy-or-so years? With technology omnipresent, an avalanche of homework, and a diminished focus on higher pursuits, teenagers are rarely encouraged nor expected to fill their free time with anything but amusement. Passion hasn't just taken a backseat in our society—it's been forgotten.

As adults, this neglect of passion translates into a disproportionate focus on employment. When did we stop thinking of career planning as finding our vocation? What is your *calling?* I shudder to think of how many college students are currently studying in fields that do not genuinely excite them. Too many think a degree is a ticket to a job, focusing solely on that destination, while ignoring the educational journey itself. The pressure to get credentialed limits the college experience to mere training rather than the special, extended opportunity to learn more about the passions in their life. Valuing financial profit above one's passions is one of the surest ways to *start* living vanilla.

In this way, college is like a career where decisions driven by passion are the ones that tend to lead to real satisfaction and success. Students will take accounting over mathematics and public relations over creative writing to train for a certain type of job they already know exists. It's tragic how many college graduates have accrued outrageous student loan debt, yet only have vanilla interests to show for it.

Whether pursuing a first job or an encore career, everyone should pause to consider what is meaningful in his or her life. Ranking these items will provide you clarity in determining your Mint Chocolate Chip Strategy.

Profit, Provision, Purpose...or Passion

In a moment, you'll return to your list of passions in the Passions Worksheet and draw a star next to the ones you can potentially parlay into your dream career—that is our primary goal here. But first you will need to consider whether a given item is really a passion or perhaps a goal or a value instead. This section will help you distinguish what's what.

We intentionally began this brainstorming process as broadly as possible, like selecting a large block of marble before knowing what the sculpture will become. So far, you have built up a big list of passions, and you have done this without a specific definition of passion. To help you chisel and prioritize your list, let's take a moment to define what a passion is *not*.

When I lead clients through this process at Stop the Vanilla LLC., their lists commonly contain items that are understandably important to them, but in this context are not actually passions. These items typically fall into three categories: profit, provision, and purpose.

Profit

Profit, to reiterate, is not considered a passion here. Certainly, you want to succeed financially, and that may even be your primary objective in career planning, but money is not a passion in and of itself. It is a result of a great strategy, with your passion providing the means to achieve it. It's more likely that wealth represents freedom to you, so what would you do if you had financial freedom? You may get a clearer idea which are your true passions by imagining what you would do if you had all the money you needed. Although the stories at the beginning of this chapter resulted in people earning a great living, and in some cases, a fortune, it only happened because they pursued a passion in their life *first*.

Provision

Providing for family is another item commonly listed here, but similar to profit, provisions, and fulfilling responsibilities, it is not a passion. There are wonderful and honorable ways to tie family values into your career, but the surest way to provide plenty for your household is to base your career around a passion. If caring for aging parents has led you to an interest in gerontology, then working with our elderly population should make your passion list. If your favorite time of the day is when your family gathers at the dinner table, perhaps your passion is connected to home cooking, and will lead you to envision a new product or service that will make dinner time special for other families as well. If divorce or home dynamics are topics that you feel strongly about, this could indicate a passion for counseling that would make you an ideal marriage and family therapist. "Family" is one of the most common items I see on the list of passions, but take note. While it's absolutely well-intentioned, ask yourself if you can build your future around it. If you can't, and if your response was more about being committed to your family or providing for your family, then don't give this one a star.

Purpose

This brings us to the third type of response that will not be starred in your list—purpose. Your purpose on the planet is likely too vast, grand, or even too general to be considered as a passion here. Highly admirable causes such as being the best parent to your child, inventing a cure for cancer, or saving a species from extinction fall more under personal missions than passions upon which to base this decision process. Think of a passion as something you love to do, such as diving into world history, and a purpose as the reason or conviction *for* your passion. **A purpose can fuel a career, but a great career is built on a passion.**

With these distinctions in mind, return now to your Passions Worksheet. Focus on what intrinsically motivates you—what you do because you find it personally enjoyable, interesting, or rewarding. In Chapter 4, we will further clarify whether a given passion can translate into career prospects, but for now, in column three of your worksheet, enter a star next to all the items you enjoy *and* could get paid to do. If you are not sure, still draw a star. Keep this list as open as possible because a creative, entrepreneurial mindset can turn just about any passion into a profit.

Although you will rack your brain as you do this work, don't forget to trust your gut. This is the first step in your plan to stop living vanilla, and while it might not have hit you yet, you'll always remember the feeling you had when it all comes together.

My Lightbulb Moment

Growing up, I never gave any thought to what my passions were, let alone how to pursue them. Raised in a lower-middle-class family with five siblings, my dreams consisted of what fun I could have when I wasn't in school or working. Right through my first year of college, planning beyond that day's responsibilities or that night's excitement was not part of my thought process.

My mindset was not uncommon. I focused on meeting basic needs, and in a word—survival. My three older siblings had all gone to college, so I followed suit, but was undeclared in my major. Beyond my general coursework, I took a few business classes because it seemed to be what people did if they wanted to make money. Meanwhile, I was on the football team, worked two part-time jobs, and was far more focused on fun than on education. I was truly just getting by, as evidenced by my stellar first-semester grade point average of 2.2!

To free up my days during sophomore year, I decided to take a night class, which was uncommon back then. It was just another marketing lecture for me, right down to my slouching behind the person in front of me so I could zone out in peace. I had no clue it would change my life. A couple classes into the course, a topic suddenly cut through the monotony. This professor was not just an academic—he taught night classes because he worked in business during the day. And in relating the lesson to his daily work, he began to speak to something that sat me right up in my chair: business strategy. How a company differentiates itself was a fascinating subject to me. Why would a person or company choose to do business with one company instead of another?

Why did that class make me pay attention like I never had before? Did the word "strategy" resonate because of how badly I needed one in my own life? Did strategic management remind me of my football playbook? Or did differentiation appeal to some desire to stand out at a crowded college? I'll never forget my vivid sensation. The entire room brightened up! It was a true epiphany—a real lightbulb moment. Strategy was *it*. Strategy was my Mint Chocolate Chip before I even knew what to call it!

That night class was just the wake-up call I needed. From then on, I completely transformed as a student and as a person. For the first time in my life, I experienced true clarity, and it drove me to succeed. Discovering my passion ignited my engagement and interest in my education, and from that pitiful 2.2 grade point average my first semester, I wound up graduating with high honors.

I share my personal story not because it's exceptional, but because it's not at all. You see, I have heard thousands of stories just like it. Every fortunate individual who loves what they do has a story of discovering their passion— their Mint Chocolate Chip—and how they turned it into a career they love.

Let's Write Your Story

You can go through less hardship and trial by error than most by being intentional *now* with how you discover your passions. By completing this self-reflection, you will arrive at new insights into what sparks your interests and enthusiasm. A single lightbulb moment can illuminate the foundation for a successful career and fulfilling life.

It's true that I felt exceptionally motivated by the powerful epiphany I experienced, but where would my passion lead me? If I had a new problem, it's that I had no direction for this excitement. I had a powerful motor with no steering wheel. And it took me *fifteen years* to figure out what to do with the passion I had discovered. I want to spare you the frustration, time, and toil. The main reason I didn't know which way I should go was that I didn't know who I was.

Once you have finalized and prioritized the passions in your life, your next step to Stop the Vanilla in Your Career and Life is to understand, own, and leverage your natural behavioral style. You need to own your cone!

The Scoop on Next Steps

Enter your prioritized passions that have a star from the Passions Worksheet in the first column of the downloadable Mint Chocolate Chip Strategy PDF, or in the Stop the Vanilla Career and Life Planning Course at Courses.StopTheVanilla.com.

3

Own the Cone

*"God grant me the serenity
To accept the things I cannot change;
Courage to change the things I can;
And wisdom to know the difference."*

— **Reinhold Niebuhr, "Serenity Prayer"**

Written in 1951, Niebuhr's words still resonate today—particularly for those of us with a vendetta against vanilla. We all have aspects of our natural behavior we wish we could change. There are personal tendencies we are less than crazy about, and they tend to lead to many misunderstandings. We cannot permanently undo, erase, nor "fix" these parts of who we are, but we do have control over our ability to accept and embrace our natural behavioral style rather than resent it. It means we acknowledge both our gifts *and* our flaws, while working to overcome the latter. And, as per Niebuhr's prayer, such a kind, yet frank appraisal of ourselves requires a level head and a serene state of mind, whether the source of that serenity is a higher power, some meditation, or a quiet walk or drive.

If the previous chapter focused on what Steve Jobs called "matters of the heart," this chapter zeroes in on a matter of the brain, which we call your natural behavioral style. Clarity is paramount if you want to stop living vanilla. This next step prescribes the clearest, most insightful look at your life. We call it your behavioral style because that is really what it is—how you behave. To enjoy your passions, excel, and live the life you want, you will need to be truthful to yourself about who you really, naturally are.

Know Yourself

Your significant other, boss, best friend, kids, direct reports—everyone has their own natural behavioral style. What exactly is yours? Too few have taken the ten-or-so minutes necessary to find out, but that meager time investment can save you a tremendous amount of time and energy later. Think about it this way. How much time have you wasted trying to be someone you aren't? Let's stop that vanilla futility.

How do you find yourself behaving in private conversations, in front of groups, or alone in a crowd? These seemingly mundane scenarios provide glimpses of a greater wisdom based in behavioral science, which is the study of your natural talents, inclinations, and communication styles. Knowing yours will make you more productive than you've ever been. Before you regret not having done this life-changing exercise sooner, focus instead on the unnecessary stress you will avoid in the future and the self-knowledge you'll gain from doing it now. If you like, spare a thought for the poor souls who will never really know themselves. As the brilliant philosopher Socrates pro-claimed, "The unexamined life is not worth living." Per-haps he could have said the vanilla life is not worth living!

As described in Chapter 2, the ice cream is a symbol for your passion, as it is sweet and exciting, but needs to be enjoyed before it melts away. The solid cone represents the unchanging, factual nature of your behavioral style, which is fully formed in your adolescent years and remains with you the rest of your life. This does not mean you can't work to improve any behavioral deficiencies. Rather, with behav-ioral science, you can identify any blind spots you have and formulate tech-niques to minimize them, if not make them work for you. But remember, you cannot overcome something if you are not aware it exists. That's why knowing your natural behavioral style is so central to living a happy and fulfilled life!

If you take away one thing from this chapter, if not this entire book, let it be the importance of understanding, owning, and leveraging your natural behavioral style. No other concept is as vital to helping you Stop the Vanilla in Your Career and Life. Unlike other career planning processes that have you choose a career path based on a feeling or what you think you like, *Stop the Vanilla in Your Career and Life* uses accurate and scientifically validated behavioral science assessments. That is why this process works.

> *If you take away one thing from this chapter, if not this entire book, let it be the importance of understanding, owning, and leveraging your natural behavioral style.*

Whatever your ideal fit may be, achieving it will require self-awareness—insight regarding your abilities *and* your limitations, and recognizing that you have incredible strengths, but blind spots as well. You can't manage something you can't see, nor can you develop something you don't understand.

Such honest awareness is integral to productive collaboration, gaining support from others, and navigating conflicts. In other words, by learning the language of your own behavioral style, you'll become more fluent in behavioral science itself. You will be able to recognize your peers' natural styles and interact with them more effectively, whether they understand it themselves or not.

DISCovering the Importance of Behavioral Science

Behavioral science has been studied, measured, discussed, and diagnosed for over a hundred years, thanks to an array of assessments and terminologies we can use. In my own career, through decades of working in talent planning and development, the most straightforward and applicable behavioral language I have worked with is called DISC.

I have found DISC to be the best assessment of its kind, whether I'm working with a company to fill a position, creating a leadership development plan, or supporting a client as they plan their future. Candidly, I only see behavioral science becoming more mainstream as people realize it will help ensure they can love what they do and live the life they want.

When you are passionate about what you do and execute it most naturally, you put yourself in prime position to succeed, to improve without limits, and to continually enjoy the increasing dividends. That is the crux of the Stop the Vanilla in Your Career and Life Process, and there's simply no ceiling to it.

As with any transformative measures, the more you put in, the more you will get out of it. And with the Stop the Vanilla in Your Career and Life Process, your effort will be rewarded exponentially after you have first completed a behavioral science assessment. This step provides objective, reliable information on your natural behavioral style, upon which you will build your successful career and life plan. You have already written out your passions, so likewise, we'll want to put your natural behavioral style into words too. The vocabulary of the DISC assessment allows us to effectively talk through specific behavioral characteristics.

DISC was developed as a tool for evaluating behavioral styles back in the early 1900s, yet to this day it has no rival. DISC measures the core aspects of human behavior, rather than trapping individuals into yes-or-no, this-or-that categories like many assessments out there today. DISC determines one's intensity in four distinct behavioral factors: Dominance, Influence, Steadiness, and Compliance. If I happen to grit my teeth when a client casually refers to DISC as a personality test, it's because it's neither a test nor a measure of personality. It's an assessment that measures behavior, which is only one aspect of one's personality. As an example, your sense of humor is part of your personality. There are no right or wrong answers with the DISC assessment—there is just a discovery of how you are *wired*.

So, how *are* you wired? How assertive are you naturally? How naturally trusting are you? How patient? How detailed? In less than fifteen minutes, a DISC assessment can measure these behavioral traits which explain how you respond to:

- Problems (Dominance)
- People (Influence)
- Pace (Steadiness)
- Procedures (Compliance)

When you go through our Career Insights/DISC assessment at Stop The Vanilla, LLC we provide your results in a clear, personalized, content-rich 15-page report.

To help you identify the greatest strengths of your natural behavioral style for column 2 of your Mint Chocolate Chip Strategy Template please carefully review all pages of the report with specific focus on the following sections:

- Personal characteristics

- Personal strengths

- Ideal work environment

Focus on your greatest strengths as identified in your behavioral science assessment and from your life experiences.

Clients often remark how incredible it feels to learn so much about themselves. It's typically a breakthrough for most people to understand their natural behavioral style for the first time. Knowledge is power!

Self-awareness of your natural behavioral style will help you experience personal breakthroughs. I would strongly encourage you to complete a DISC behavioral science assessment to increase the effectiveness of this process. If you are interested in learning more about your style and wish to purchase reliable and comprehensive behavioral science assessments and results, simply email us at Info@StopTheVanilla.com.

Once you understand your natural behavioral style, next you will work to own it, and finally, you will be able to leverage your style to work in your favor. These three steps—understand, own, and leverage—will lead you to loving what you do to live the life you want.

Every behavioral style imaginable can lead to success.

Understand It

It is essential to have self-awareness before you can bring value to others, let alone lead them. In fact, you will find few problems in life that are not created from a lack of personal understanding. Keep the focus on your career for now, though, and you will see how many other facets of your life will fall into place once you are passionate about your daily work.

What are the strengths of your natural behavioral style that you can wrap your career around? Where do you bring the greatest value to a project, an organization or team, and to yourself? What are the blind spots and growth opportunities of your style that you need to work on? Knowing your own style helps you understand how it impacts other styles, which leads to healthier relationships. Understanding and taking advantage of the strengths of your natural behavior will set you up for success.

The exciting benefits of owning and leveraging your natural behavioral style await you, not to mention the self-discovery might lead to mind-blowing breakthroughs. I see this happen often in development sessions, and it's nearly as moving for me as it is for the individuals themselves. Their energy hits new heights with the new knowledge, as if suddenly and clearly their path away from living vanilla has been revealed. You too stand to experience personal and professional revelations by understanding your natural behavioral style.

I hope you'll make plans to take the DISC assessment, but for now, let us complete a quick overview of the dimensions of DISC. Natural behavior can be broken down into four major components and defining these terms will help you understand your unique style.

D is for Dominance

How do you respond to challenges and conflict? Do you step back and pause to think things through, or are you instantly activated, and inspired to reframe from reaction to action? The public persona of LeBron James exhibits strong Dominance characteristics.

People with high-Dominance assessment scores tend to be decisive, aggressive, and forceful. In the context of an organization, I call them the gas pedals—the people always pushing the team or project forward. They are ambitious, independent, and confident, with a high desire to win. They are also good problem solvers who are bottom-line oriented. People with high Dominance typically have very active minds that generate a lot of creative and visionary ideas. Their value comes in their ability to initiate activity, challenge the status quo, and maintain a forward-looking perspective with an entrepreneurial mindset. In a sales position, those with strong Dominance have the fortitude to open new doors, close the toughest of sales, and bring in new business.

However, those with high Dominance also tend to have shorter attention spans and lose interest in projects after the initial challenge fades. They may lack tact, not recognize the different behavioral styles around them, overshadow peers, and overstep authority; not because they are rude, but because it's simply how they are wired. They may also have a shorter wick on their temper and may show anger more readily than the other three styles.

For each dimension of DISC, your score can range from high to low. The higher or lower the score, the more intensity in that factor. The low measurement of Dominance suggests a more reflective and laid-back demeanor. People with low Dominance scores tend to take a more cautious approach and are conservative by nature. They are more agreeable, peaceful, and have a longer fuse. Those with low levels of Dominance are easy to get along with but may be uncomfortable having the tough conversations, holding others accountable, and standing up for or defending their beliefs.

I is for Influence

How do you influence others to your point of view? The Influence characteristic displays an introverted style on the low end and an extroverted style on the high end. The public persona of Will Ferrell exhibits high Influence characteristics.

People with high Influence scores tend to sway others with their verbal skills and warmth. They love to interact, are usually popular, and want people to like them. They are very trusting, optimistic, and articulate. Those with high Influence scores have an ability to be conversational, open-minded, convincing, and enthusiastic while being personable—they are great at "working the room." Their value lies in building relationships and rapport quickly and motivating others toward goals. They have a positive sense of humor and negotiate conflict well.

However, an individual high in Influence may rely too much on verbal communication and not pay enough attention to details. They often struggle with time management, plan poorly, and act impulsively. They do not always listen well and will rely more on emotion and gut feeling than facts, which can get them in trouble. They tend to trust indiscriminately, and their problem-solving approach is to be appeasing.

On the other end of the spectrum, people with low Influence scores tend to be more introverted, reserved, and calculated. The lower the score, the more intense these characteristics are. They rely more on facts than charm to exert influence. Those with low Influence levels are typically skeptical of others. For them, trust grows over time.

S is for Steadiness

How do you respond to the pace of your environment? The Steadiness characteristic reveals a fast-paced comfort zone on the low end and a more methodical approach on the high end. The public persona of Carrie Underwood exhibits high Steadiness characteristics.

People with high Steadiness scores tend to listen well to others and like to serve, which makes them great team players. They prefer to focus on one or two tasks at a time, because they appreciate closure and are driven to finish what they start. High Steadiness individuals are measured, loyal people, and often appear relaxed even if they are not. Other natural strengths for this style are patience, empathy, and logic. Those with high Steadiness are very engaged when working for a leader and a cause they believe in. They are dependable, good at reconciling factions, and can calm others down. They would rather have a few deep friendships versus a lot of acquaintances.

However, individuals with high Steadiness appear to have little sense of urgency, will internalize others' comments, take criticism of their work personally, carry grudges in a mental backpack, and can be resistant to change. Their approach to problem-solving is observing, reflecting, and avoiding.

The flip side of Steadiness are those who score low in this category. These individuals are comfortable multitasking. They adapt quickly to change and prefer a fast-paced work environment. The lower the score, the faster pace they have. Efficiency is of the utmost importance in moving projects forward. Those with low scores in Steadiness tend to be impatient, intense, impulsive, and restless, often struggling to listen and focus on detailed work for a long period of time.

C is for Compliance

How do you respond to rules, details, and systems? A low measurement of Compliance shows low attention to detail, while a high measurement of Compliance predicts a high attention to detail, accuracy, and/or quality. The public persona of Bill Belichick exhibits high Compliance characteristics.

People with high Compliance scores tend to be precise, technical, analytical, and systems-oriented. They have a high attention to detail and love collecting data. They are thinkers, ask great questions, and focus on quality. High Compliance individuals are often the expert in the room. Their value lies in their ability to think objectively, and the high standards they maintain. They are task-oriented and feel most comfortable clarifying, gathering information, criticizing, and testing.

However, high Compliance limitations include being worrisome and exacting, which leads them on a longer path to making decisions. Their high standards often lead to them being harsh on themselves and others. They tend to get lost in the details and avoid risk. They evaluate, plan, and investigate, and can come across to others as overly critical.

People with low Compliance scores can be independent, avoid detail work, and are more comfortable with risk. The lower the score, the more risk they may take. They are willing to make decisions without having all of the information and to break rules and procedures when they see fit.

To learn more about the strengths and limitations of each behavioral characteristic, you can watch a video at StopTheVanilla.com/Assessments or in the Stop the Vanilla Career and Life Planning Course at Courses.StopTheVanilla.com.

The DISC comparison chart below provides an excellent summary of the key characteristics. In general, those with higher Influence and Steadiness tend to be more people-oriented, while those with higher Dominance and Compliance tend to be more task and results-oriented.

DISC Behavioral Style Comparison Chart

	D	I	S	C
Primary Need	To Direct	To Interact	To Support	To Comply
Primary Emotion	Anger	Optimism	Non-emotion	Fear
Takes Pride in Dealing With	Problems / Challenges	People / Contacts	Pace / Consistency	Procedures / Constraints
Orientation	Task	People	People	Task
Focus	External	External	Internal	Internal
Under Stress	Impatient	Disorganized	Possessive	Critical
Emphasis Is	Results / Efficiency	Fun / Experience	Trust	Procedures / Information
Distinguishing Qualities	Dominant	Influencer	Steady	Compliant

To provide you with a high-level understanding of the strongest characteristics of your own natural behavioral style (DISC), take a few minutes to review the following descriptors of each characteristic:

- If the following descriptors portray you, you will likely score **high in Dominance**:
  - Decisive
  - Aggressive
  - Problem solver
  - Ambitious
  - Confident
- If the following descriptors portray you, you will likely score **low in Dominance**:
  - Cautious
  - Conservative
  - Agreeable
  - Laid back
  - Slow to anger
- If the following descriptors portray you, you will likely score **high in Influence**:
  - Trusting
  - Optimistic
  - Outgoing
  - Convincing
  - Enthusiastic
- If the following descriptors portray you, you will likely score **low in Influence**:
  - Introverted
  - Reserved
  - Calculating

- o Skeptical
- o Non-emotional
- If the following descriptors portray you, you will likely score **high in Steadiness**:
  - o Loyal
  - o Relaxed
  - o Patient
  - o Empathetic
  - o Team player
- If the following descriptors portray you, you will likely score **low in Steadiness**:
  - o Fast-paced
  - o Efficient
  - o Impatient
  - o Impulsive
  - o Multi-tasker
- If the following descriptors portray you, you will likely score **high in Compliance**:
  - o Accurate
  - o Technical/Expert
  - o Systems-oriented
  - o Detailed
  - o Objective
- If the following descriptors portray you, you will likely score **low in Compliance**:
  - o Independent

- ○ Avoids detailed work
- ○ Comfortable with risk
- ○ Makes decisions without all the information
- ○ Rule-breaker

What have you learned about yourself so far? It is important to know this is just the tip of the iceberg compared to a detailed assessment and report. It's amazing to see what happens to a person when they begin to learn about themselves in a way they never have before! While there is a high and low for each behavioral style, there are many subtle but important nuances we can discover in the results.

It is even more important to remember that all natural behavioral styles have strengths and weaknesses, bring equal value to a team and organization, and once understood and owned, can be leveraged to live a passionate and rewarding life.

Any style can do any job, but certain styles are more comfortable in certain positions.

People with high Compliance, for example, are typically very comfortable in accounting careers. Comfort in a position leads to higher performance, and therefore higher enjoyment, so what type of career will be most comfortable for *your* natural behavioral style? If you are already deep into your career, does it make more sense as to why certain tasks or aspects of your job are draining while others are energizing?

Adaptive Style

Some people behave just about the same at home as they do at work. However, others need to switch gears entirely to be successful at their jobs, which requires them to behave different as soon as they "punch in." This behavioral phenomenon is called **adaption**. In most cases, adaption is not even a conscious effort. While some people may not realize the degree to which they are adapting for a job, they will eventually feel it.

For example, the graphs below show this person is adapting their Influence factor down 20 points from 58 to 38 at work.

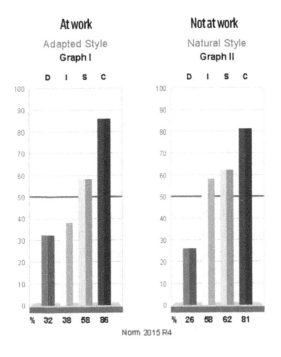

Beware of Significant Adaption

It takes a great deal of energy to adapt one's style, and doing so long-term can cause a great deal of stress and fatigue. Imagine an introvert having to be the point person on sales calls, for example, or an extrovert having to sit quietly in a cubicle all day!

While we are all capable of swimming against our behavioral currents, it's excessive adaption at work that leads to job discontentment and ultimately burnout. Adapting in the moment to have a healthy interaction is a good thing, as you are communicating to the other person the way they want to be communicated to. But adapting your style over the long term is unhealthy and will take its toll. The start of adaption is when any DISC characteristic in your adaptive style changes by more than ten compared to that same characteristic in your natural style. A change greater than twenty is significant adaption, and that's when it will start to affect you adversely.

Some people can adapt their styles in the short term without suffering too much, but everyone will feel better in a career that fits their natural style. We call that alignment or "being home."

Most people who adapt significantly at work already know their job takes a lot out of them. They are often drained by the end of the week, but think their exhaustion is from simply working so hard. When we explain the concept of adapting your style at work to them, something clicks. They begin to realize why their current position wears them out and are truly excited to stop living vanilla and get back to something that is more natural for them.

Own It

Did you get to pick your parents? Obviously not. Nor, for example, did you get the opportunity to decide if you wanted to be an introvert or an extrovert. You also did not get to choose your natural behavioral style, but you will need to own it to live the life of your choice.

It may help you to know your natural behavioral style was heavily influenced by factors beyond your control, such as genetics, your birth order, and how your parents raised you. Nonetheless, behavioral science results are not always easy to accept. We all have attributes to our styles that we do not always like—things we would want to change about ourselves if we could. A significant step in the art of "owning the cone" is overcoming what we call *style envy*—the desire to be like others—where we envy those who are more naturally outgoing, organized, or one of many other traits we tend to admire in others.

Rather than dwell on or feel trapped by assessment results, let them free you. Like the "Serenity Prayer," you can utilize this self-knowledge to stop wasting energy on something you did not create and cannot alter. Once you have allowed yourself to accept and embrace your natural behavioral style—strengths, weaknesses, all of it—you'll have moved closer to a rich, fulfilling, and flavorful life.

It's useful to assess and acknowledge our capabilities, and there's also virtue and honesty in doing so. We all have issues, and if someone tells you they don't, that is their first issue. The beauty is there is no shame *or* pride in the results of a DISC assessment—nothing to be bashful *or* to brag about. Behavioral assessments remove emotion and bias from the way you'll view and talk about yourself,

> *We all have issues and if someone tells you they don't, that is their first issue.*

describing your natural style as a fact and science instead of a feeling or opinion, thereby providing genuine clarity of self.

When you make a mistake because of your natural behavioral style—which you inevitably will—you will need to own it, apologize for it, learn from it, and move on. Making things right when your natural behavioral style's gotten the best of you can be the hardest part of owning it. If you do not own your style, though, you'll fail to resolve a little issue that will grow and take root until suddenly it requires significant work to resolve.

Owning your unique natural style is a critical step, and it isn't always easy. It's unfortunately common for people to stall at this step and experience what I call *style denial*. Over the long term, it is only natural that we'll revert back to being our natural selves. Why fight it, then, when you can make it fight for you?

Transparency

Behavioral science allows us to talk about topics we may not have known about, have been unable to talk about, or have covered up. A new level of transparency about your natural style will bring you strength instead of shame. Once you own your weaknesses as part of your natural behavior, you can effectively wield them, moving you from defensiveness to development.

As vulnerable and perhaps unintuitive as that may feel, know that **transparency is the foundation of humility, and perhaps the single greatest key to a life of growth and fulfilling relationships.** One of the best ways to achieve transparency in a relationship is to offer it yourself first. When a leader is transparent and honest, other people want to follow. Humble transparency makes someone more coachable and a greater contributor to your high-performance environment. Clear communication earns the ability to resolve the sensitive issues with candor and respect. It also improves the delegation of tasks based on individual strengths and weaknesses. People love to work with a leader who understands and appreciates what each team member brings to the team.

They say sunlight is the single greatest disinfectant, because we can only do something about it once it's brought to light. In owning your style, you admit there are deficiencies that you can now take action to minimize. What a great feeling! You have not given yourself a pass for, say, poor listening tendencies, but rather acknowledged specific skills you'll need to work to develop. This awareness leads to more grace for yourself in scenarios where you are not a natural expert but are striving to improve.

It's endearing to others, too. Transparency allows you to have deeper conversations and build healthier relationships—it's amazing how comfortably and quickly communication will progress when you admit something real about your style to someone else. Sharing your behavioral style results with any person will always improve that relationship. The better we understand someone, the more we can effectively communicate with them.

After realizing my passion for strategy, I excelled through my undergraduate degree, earned my MBA in Strategic Management, and experienced immediate career success. However, my growing confidence soon verged on arrogance and even aggression, to where anyone who disagreed with me was clearly wrong—according to me. Then, a company I worked with began to use behavioral science to aid in hiring applicants, and I had to take an assessment myself—not because I wanted to, but to see what type of tools we were working with. The assessment led to a sudden, brutal realization: This know-it-all was in fact pretty clueless. **When I discovered my natural behavioral style at the age of thirty-five, it felt like the first day of the rest of my life.**

Steve

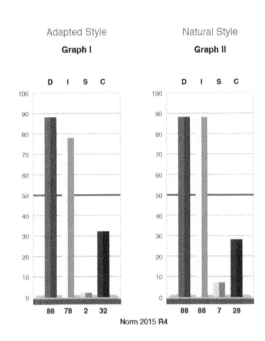

Adapted Style
Graph I

Natural Style
Graph II

It would take yours truly *years* to work through and own my style (high Dominance and low Steadiness). For example, my mind works at a very fast pace, and to put it mildly, I struggle to stay listening for long stretches of time. Knowing this and becoming aware of its impact, I learned to use a technique I call "listening with my eyes." When talking to another person I look them in the eyes to stay focused on listening. Another technique I use is to consciously modify my pace to match the pace of others.

It's been tremendously humbling, but also good to know that any discomfort I experience in owning my weaknesses and flaws is worthwhile—a step backward for the sake of a big jump ahead! As I began to understand the benefits of clarity of self, the clarity only increased. Further, my newfound transparency was picked up on, recognized, and appreciated by those I spend the most time with: my family and co-workers.

Understanding and owning your style will improve every relationship in your life!

Leverage It

Once you have understood and owned your natural behavioral style, you are ready to leverage it. This is where the real fun picks up. Beyond the immediate benefits of transparency, the best way to leverage your style is to wrap it around one of the passions in your life—to do what you love, love what you do, and be the best at it. This is what the Stop the Vanilla in Your Career and Life Process is all about.

Now that you have taken a significant step in understanding and owning yours, please use the results of your behavioral science report and/or your life experiences in listing the top strengths of your natural style.

Here is my personal list as an example for you:

1) Visionary thinker
2) Action-oriented
3) Communicator
4) Comfortable in front of the room
5) Problem solver
6) Gets things done
7) Creates helpful methodologies and processes

List your strengths here:

_____

_____

_____

_____

_____

_____

_____

_____

Now, how will you utilize your strengths? In the next chapter you will work on leveraging them into a successful career, and you will brainstorm career options where the strengths of your style intersect with the passions in your life. We will combine what you have accomplished and unearthed in these last two chapters and formulate your personalized Mint Chocolate Chip Strategy. Please know that if you are already well into your career, this can be the first day of the rest of your life, as it was mine. You can make adjustments that will create much greater satisfaction in your career and life, or you can make more significant changes that will make for a better fit long term. Either way, I'm excited for this journey of self-discovery and hope you are too!

These first two steps—identifying your passions and your natural behavioral strengths—have given you a lot to digest! You have made real progress, and I hope you are already benefitting from the clarity you've gained. I assure you the real sweet stuff is yet to come!

The Scoop on Next Steps

- Contact us at Info@StoptheVanilla.com to purchase DISC and other behavioral science assessments.

- Using your assessment results and life experiences, enter your greatest strengths into the second column in the downloadable Mint Chocolate Chip Strategy PDF or in the Stop the Vanilla Career and Life Planning Course at Courses.StopTheVanilla.com.

4

Sweet Options

"Wealth is not about having a lot of money;
it's about having a lot of options."

—Chris Rock

Premise 1: Ice cream is a go-to indulgence for stress relief.

Premise 2: Indecision is a major source of stress.

Question: Why, then, would ice cream chain, Baskin-Robbins famously give us "31 flavors" to choose from?

Answer: As wise Mr. Rock astutely observes, we appreciate the wealth of options and the luxury of choosing for ourselves. We value freedom of choice. In other words, we crave the opportunity to select the one flavor we want most, *more* than we agonize from missing out on the other thirty.

Don't Be Afraid to Sample

Thankfully, most ice cream parlors are kind enough to let customers sample the different flavors. Sometimes all we need is a small taste to satisfy our curiosity and help us make up our minds. This is where you're at in the Stop the Vanilla in Your Career and Life Process—contemplating career options that occur where the passions in your life intersect with the strengths of your natural behavioral style.

Even if you think they are out of reach at the moment, consider all the possible career options that are at this intersection of loving what you do and doing it naturally.

This chapter combines your work from the previous two, preparing you to create *your* Mint Chocolate Chip Strategy.

Does the prospect of making that decision fill you with excitement, or give you a pinch of anxiety? Whether you identify as a control freak, have a "helicopter" parent who wants to make your decisions for you, feel like you are having a mid-life crisis, or have a habit of passively accepting whatever life hands you, this chapter will leave you comfortable—if not eager—to choose the path that leads to living out your passion, no matter where you're currently at in your career.

> *Clarity is not beside or behind you. It's in front of you.*

The Right Time to Treat Yourself

If you naturally struggle to pull the trigger on large decisions, the way high-Compliance behavioral styles do, for example, then here is an easy one. In the face of uncertainty, choose to pursue your passions. **It is never too late to stop living a vanilla life.**

Readers who are further along in your careers, while your options may feel limited by time, you have the invaluable advantage of experience. You will be especially wise with your time going forward because you appreciate and understand its value, not to mention you'll be more apt to maximize your time thanks to the perspective you've gained. And despite your fiscal responsibilities, you're also more likely to have more expendable income or savings to explore options for your next career move. Regardless of your age, why waste another day doing what you do not want to do? My most common advice for individuals further along in their careers is that there's no time like the present to pursue a more fulfilling career. I agree with Martin Luther's timeless statement: "Even if I knew that tomorrow the world would go to pieces, I would still plant my apple tree."

For those of you who are earlier in your career, the challenge in choosing your path is a bit different. You are probably worried about limiting yourself, but you cannot pursue everything, even if you have more time to figure things out. Your greatest assets, though, are how few major responsibilities you may have at this stage in your life, such as dependents, mortgages, or elderly parents. These factors should increase your willingness to take risks, sample different career fields, and/or relocate. Keep moving forward, constantly search and research via experiments and experience, and continue to zero in on a winning life strategy. If the process has begun to feel overwhelming, recall how much work you have already done. It's worth it!

Not Starting from Scratch

All of us have the recipe for our own Mint Chocolate Chip Strategy within us, and you have already identified your two key ingredients: your passions and your natural behavioral style. Before pinpointing these, you, like most people, probably struggled to answer that eternal inquiry: *What do I want to do with my life?*

You have hopefully learned by now that you're closer to answering that question than you may have thought, that your slate is not so blank, and that your dream career is within reach.

But which option for your dream job will you reach for, and how? Deciding which passion to wrap your style around, and choosing or creating a career for your hierarchy of needs will take focus and persistence. For some, the path reveals itself instantly; for others, the path can take some time to come together—more an evolution than a revolution. As I tell my clients, clarity is not beside or behind you, but in front of you. When you keep stepping toward your passion, you will evolve, gain clarity, and break free from a vanilla life.

Odds in Your Flavor

By defining your passions, you have already increased your chances of living them—you are no longer "aiming for nothing" as the late Zig Ziglar would say. Don't rely on fate or luck to find your plan for success, because your odds for success are even greater when you intentionally pursue your passions. What follows are three examples of people who stumbled into living their passions.

As a young boy, Guy Laliberté discovered his passion for show business after his parents took him to the circus. Inspired, Laliberté began performing his own rudimentary routines in the street after school, improving and honing his craft for tips and applause through his teens. Conventional wisdom convinced Laliberté he would need to abandon his childhood passion and just plain grow up, so he took a full-time job at a hydroelectric dam. Shortly after, though, the company's employees went on strike. Thankfully, Laliberté had not yet extinguished his love for entertaining, and he rounded up some performers he knew to start a new troupe. He called it Cirque du Soleil, and about twenty-five years later, this entertainment company generates over $800 million in annual revenue. Laliberté lives his passion today because he never fully abandoned his pursuit of it.

Oprah Winfrey is one of the most famous American media personalities today, greatly admired for her remarkable, unlikely ascent out of childhood poverty and abuse. Perhaps as a distraction from her daily hardship, young Winfrey would playfully conduct imaginary interviews with animals she would come across, as well as the few toys she possessed. This hobby alone did not lead to her big break, though. Rather, Winfrey just happened to enter, and win, a beauty contest in her teens, which then happened to catch the attention of a local radio station, kicking off one of the most successful media careers in history.

Implausible fortune would also shine upon Ralph Lifshitz. He was born in Brooklyn, the youngest of four, to Belarusian immigrants. Growing up poor, Ralph identified nice clothing as a means to gain respect. After a few years in the army, he was drawn to working as a clerk at a men's formalwear store, where his creative dreams began to run wild. Imagining his own designs for neckties, Lifshitz asked his employer if he could sell his own line of ties out of a single drawer. His ties sold well, and his business-within-a-business picked up, prompting him to pursue his passion full-time. He changed his name, continued to expand, and today, Ralph Lauren's Polo brand has made him one of the one hundred wealthiest people in the world, all because he pursued his passion.

These three incredibly successful people have stories as miraculous as they are improbable. You, however, have an advantage that none of them had! You have found clarity on your passions and behavioral style. Only in retrospect would Oprah Winfrey's grandmother say she wasn't surprised Oprah found a career in media. There was no foresight there, and certainly no one to note her penchant for imaginary interviews. Guy Laliberté and Ralph Lifshitz (Ralph Lauren) may have spared themselves years of unnecessary employment and deployment had they pursued their passions and understood their natural behavioral style right from the start. All three of them essentially started from scratch and wound up living out their passion.

My Mint Chocolate Chip Strategy

Like the stories above, my Mint Chocolate Chip Strategy came together by accident as well. At age 21 I discovered my passion for strategy, but did not take a behavioral science assessment to understand my natural behavioral style until I was 35 years old. While looking for my next career opportunity, I started helping some companies with their strategic planning process. I found leading a team through a thoughtful strategy development process came naturally to me and I absolutely loved it. After three months of taste-testing different career options that wrapped my natural style around my passion for strategy, I had accidently uncovered my Mint Chocolate Chip Strategy as a Strategy and Talent Thought Leader/Advisor/Speaker/Author.

However, *you* have an opportunity to succeed more deliberately. By crafting your Mint Chocolate Chip Strategy, you won't need to leave so much to chance. Though everyone benefits from a lucky break, creating a great strategy is like granting that break to yourself by getting you closer to your passion and becoming better positioned to be in the right place at the right time.

To get in the right frame of mind, picture yourself outside on a sweltering, cloudless Saturday afternoon—the hottest day of the summer. You stiffly stand up and arch your back after an hour of yard work, finally peeling off those sweaty gardening gloves. The sound of cicadas screaming in the trees is suddenly broken, cut through by the bright music of an ice cream truck down your street. Sweet serendipity on wheels, heading toward your house, and boy, you have earned it! Your imagination runs wild. Do I want something minty, fruity, sweet, all chocolate, or maybe even peanut butter? It all sounds so good!

That is how wide open your brainstorming should be. There are no bad ideas for this next step, so do not limit yourself. Any number of your options can be satisfying and refreshing. Be curious and aim to keep this enjoyable, as you are not committing to anything yet, just upping your odds for success.

How can you wrap your natural behavioral style around a passion in your life? Take the popular passion of sports as an example. If you are an exceptionally gifted and driven athlete, then you are likely already pursuing your sport as a career choice. If you're very passionate about sports—you devote your free time to attending and watching games, researching statistics, studying highlights—but you're not quite talented enough to earn a living from personally playing, then you might be a great fit to work in sports management or sports journalism. Now if you have a high-Dominance and high-Influence behavioral style, a worthy Mint Chocolate Chip Strategy could be a career as an agent for NFL players, where you'd live your passion for sports by wrapping it in your naturally charismatic style and ability to persuade and negotiate.

But if your style is more of high Steadiness and high Compliance, your natural demeanor, attention to detail, and technical expertise could make you an ideal fit for a role in player finance and administration, drafting contracts, and salary cap management.

If those hypothetical examples got your gears turning, the following real-life stories should set off some real brainstorming. We've included a story for each behavioral style in the DISC order, starting with high Dominance, so one of them will resonate with your style. Keep your own passions and natural behavioral style in mind as you read about real people pursuing options from the intersections of their varied styles and passions.

High Dominance: Aaron

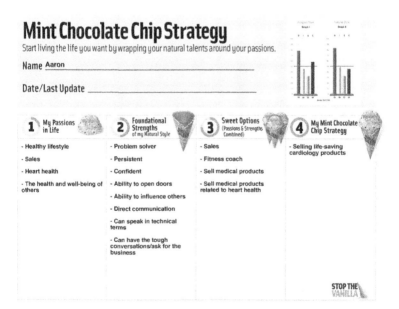

Mint Chocolate Chip Strategy
Start living the life you want by wrapping your natural talents around your passions.

Name **Aaron**

Date/Last Update _____

1 My Passions in Life	2 Foundational Strengths of my Natural Style	3 Sweet Options (Passions & Strengths Combined)	4 My Mint Chocolate Chip Strategy
- Healthy lifestyle	- Problem solver	- Sales	- Selling life-saving cardiology products
- Sales	- Persistent	- Fitness coach	
- Heart health	- Confident	- Sell medical products	
- The health and well-being of others	- Ability to open doors	- Sell medical products related to heart health	
	- Ability to influence others		
	- Direct communication		
	- Can speak in technical terms		
	- Can have the tough conversations/ask for the business		

STOP THE VANILLA

67

Aaron always had a knack for sales—not uncommon for high Dominance individuals. He is a very confident young man, especially when he believes in the product or service he's selling. Aaron's relative lack of patience becomes a strength as soon as he realizes someone needs something. He gains a sense of urgency to provide a solution, his brain firing with different approaches for his would-be customer, like a chess player ready to counter an opponent's moves. And he derives these valuable skills from his natural behavioral style as illustrated below.

Aaron

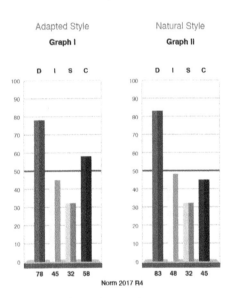

Passions are often driven by our interests, curiosities, and pleasures, but in some cases, they are informed by tragedies. As a teenager Aaron's world was all but shattered when his forty-year-old father died of a heart attack.

Such a loss motivates people to be more conscious of their health and adopt a better lifestyle. Aaron, though, wanted to take it a step further. Not only did he become more focused on his own wellbeing, he also grew passionate about helping others take better care of themselves so their loved ones would not have to experience tragic and unexpected loss like he did.

A passion for health care can lead to studying anatomy and physiology or a strong interest in working with patients, but neither of those came naturally to Aaron. Into adulthood, he worked through a variety of different sales jobs unrelated to his passion—newspaper subscriptions, cars, insurance, etc. He always excelled, but always lost interest. The work just was not meaningful beyond the initial challenge and thrill of selling something new.

That was the case until he found a way to link the strengths of his style with his passion to help heart patients survive. From his experience and networking in sales, aimless as it may have felt, Aaron wound up connecting with a pharmaceutical sales coach who worked in the heart disease industry. That was *it*! He had identified the perfect way to wrap it all together.

Aaron's lightbulb lit up brighter than ever. Having discovered his Mint Chocolate Chip Strategy, he now lives his passion, helping treat heart conditions and sparing others from tragedy by selling life-saving products such as heart monitors and stents.

High Influence: Brittany

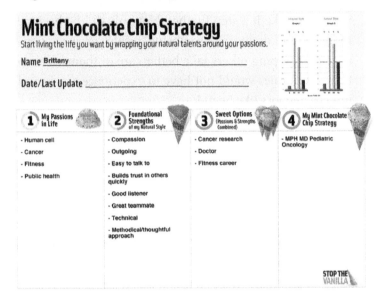

I've guided each of my four children through the Stop the Vanilla in Your Career and Life Process and I can't recommend highly enough that all parents do the same. Following is the story of our oldest, and it helped me formulate this process that has since improved countless lives.

When my daughter, Brittany, was in eighth grade, she was doing homework at the dinner table when she suddenly paused and looked up, her face glowing, as if she had just discovered buried treasure. And in a sense, she had. Britt's young mind had just been electrified by the pages of her biology textbook, and more specifically, the awesome nature of the human cell.

I always urge parents to pay close attention to these magic moments and make note of any spark that could ultimately light up their child's life. Sometimes, though, they are impossible to ignore—some kids will fixate so deeply on a passion that it becomes their sole interest, their obsession, and the only thing they want to talk about. This was absolutely the case with Britt and the human cell, as she excitedly shared her latest learning with anyone and everyone who would listen.

My wife and I fostered and encouraged this newfound passion, and it held Britt's interest through high school like a magnet. It was a foregone conclusion she would go to college and study the human cell in one way or another, but to which type of career would it lead? We were not sure. She had multiple options in science and/or medicine, but she would need to find one that fit with her high Influence style, which was revealed when she completed a DISC behavioral assessment in tenth grade.

Why is tenth grade the optimal age to complete a behavioral assessment and start career planning?

- *Freshman year in high school is a new environment, and a learning process just in itself.*

- *It can influence junior and senior year coursework and activities.*

- *It allows three years to formulate the optimum career plan by graduation.*

In trying to discover the best way to live her passion, Britt seized an incredible opportunity through her college: a three-month internship in cancer research. She could not believe it!

It was a big-league opportunity. That's why Britt was utterly shocked to discover that research was not a great fit for her. Being in a laboratory all day meant minimal contact with people, which did not harmonize with her naturally social, outgoing behavioral style. After completing her internship, the experience left Britt certain she wanted to work in direct contact with patients—to be a doctor. She learned this valuable insight but needed to dig further, since there are many different types of doctors.

Britt's DISC assessment results were invaluable to this process. Reviewing her report from highest to lowest, she and I first talked about her high Influence score, and how her genuine, optimistic nature makes her likable and trustworthy—an obviously valuable trait for a doctor. We then discussed her high Steadiness score, which accounts for her compassionate, methodical approach, and great listening skills. Britt's higher Compliance score indicated she could become an expert in her chosen field of medicine.

Brittany

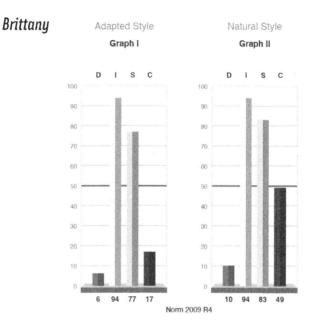

Adapted Style
Graph I

Natural Style
Graph II

6 94 77 17   10 94 83 49

Norm 2009 R4

Then, we came to her very low Dominance score. Talking through the implications, Britt suddenly realized her style was not naturally comfortable to the high-pressure decisions she would face as an emergency room doctor or a surgeon. Armed with that awareness, she continued her well-rounded studies, determined there would be a place for her in medicine. Medical schools generally aim to keep students open-minded about which field or occupation they will best fit, so she knew she had time.

As part of her ongoing research, Britt's next opportunity was to shadow a pediatric oncologist, and just like that, on went the lightbulb! Britt knew childhood oncology would be the optimal path to pursue her passion for the human cell and to do her part to protect it from cancer!

Dad, on the other hand, had reservations. "Britt," I appealed. "Are you *really* going to be able to tell people they're going to die?"

"No, Dad," she replied. "I'm going to tell them they're going to *live!*"

Her response stopped me in my tracks; it was obvious my daughter had found her Mint Chocolate Chip Strategy.

High Steadiness: Mackenzie

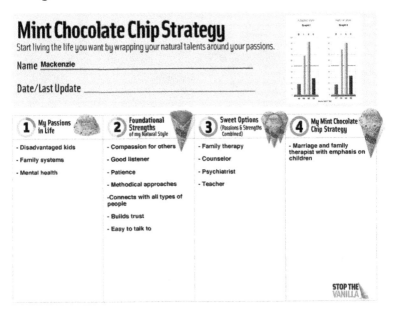

Mint Chocolate Chip Strategy

Start living the life you want by wrapping your natural talents around your passions.

Name Mackenzie

Date/Last Update

1 My Passions in Life	2 Foundational Strengths of my Natural Style	3 Sweet Options (Passions & Strengths Combined)	4 My Mint Chocolate Chip Strategy
- Disadvantaged kids	- Compassion for others	- Family therapy	- Marriage and family therapist with emphasis on children
- Family systems	- Good listener	- Counselor	
- Mental health	- Patience	- Psychiatrist	
	- Methodical approaches	- Teacher	
	-Connects with all types of people		
	- Builds trust		
	- Easy to talk to		

STOP THE VANILLA

Mackenzie described her childhood as a household with parents who raised her with love and encouragement. This childhood was the only way of life she knew. She was unaware of the challenges other kids faced in their unique family situations.

As Mackenzie's worldview broadened throughout her teens, she became aware of juvenile disadvantages that she could barely comprehend. She gained greater perspective and appreciation for how fortunate she had been, and it moved her. Mackenzie wanted to support children in the circumstances they were born into. She wanted to know what was at the root of this suffering that impacted so many lives.

Heading into college, Mackenzie's passion for supporting disadvantaged youth led her, at first, to pursue a degree in education. She soon realized, though, that she wanted to help young people on a more emotional level as opposed to teaching them English or Math. She continued her general education coursework, making necessary progress for whichever degree she would ultimately choose. After two semesters, Mackenzie was spinning her wheels instead of moving forward. She met with me shortly after she had switched her major to undeclared—a telltale sign that vanilla roots were taking hold.

Mackenzie was eager to try the process and from her DISC behavioral assessment, we quickly confirmed she has ranked very high in Steadiness. Her greatest natural behavioral strengths are her compassion, listening skills, patience, and methodical approach to resolving challenges in the lives of others. The behavioral science assessment report explained how Mackenzie is better suited for listening rather than instructing, which helped her make greater sense of her decision to not become a teacher.

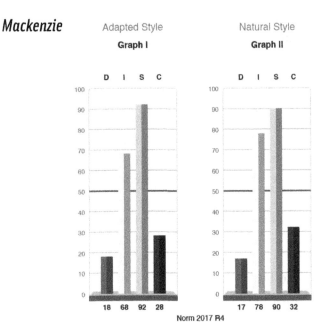

Mackenzie   Adapted Style   Natural Style

Graph I   **Graph II**

18   68   92   28   17   78   90   32

Norm 2017 R4

In her pursuit of a more natural fit for her passion, Mackenzie took a part-time job at a local psychiatric center. It was there that she discovered the importance of the family on a child's well-being, which led to the career path of family therapy. Knowing she had found the intersection of her behavior style and her passion, Mackenzie switched her major for the last time. She completed her master's degree and is now fulfilling her Mint Chocolate Chip Strategy as a Marriage and Family Therapist with an emphasis on children.

High Compliance: Jacob

Mint Chocolate Chip Strategy
Start living the life you want by wrapping your natural talents around your passions.

Name Jacob

Date/Last Update

1 My Passions in Life
- Food
- Cooking
- Spanish
- Farming
- Sustainability
- Responsible serving
- Connecting with guests

2 Foundational Strengths of my Natural Style
- Detail Orientation/technical
- Ability to become an expert in his field/craft
- Get it done right the first time
- Likes to follow a proven process
- Strong team member

3 Sweet Options (Passions & Strengths Combined)
- Waiter
- Chef
- Own a restaurant

4 My Mint Chocolate Chip Strategy
- Chef/restaurateur

STOP THE VANILLA

Jacob was born into financial stability and blessed to be able to pursue any career path he wanted, so it confounded his parents when he could not shake his passion for working with food. They explained that business would be a much wiser and more profitable career choice and discouraged him from pursuing anything culinary. They were correct in assessing Jacob as a highly-competent young man, but taking a job just for the money would never be his priority—he wanted to love what he did for a living. Why didn't anyone care?

To please just about everyone but himself, Jacob reluctantly enrolled in business and accounting classes.

Meanwhile, he thoroughly enjoyed his part-time job as a waiter at his friend's restaurant. Simply working around food was thrilling for Jacob. He was inspired by the presentation of the meals and learning what the customers liked or disliked.

Jacob's grades, meanwhile, were slipping. Without clarity for his future, he lacked motivation and focus, and was—in a word—disconnecting. It was at this time that his concerned father put Jacob in touch with me to complete the Stop the Vanilla in Your Career and Life Process.

Jacob was not exactly enthusiastic at first. When I walked into my first meeting with Jacob, he was barely sitting upright in his chair. He had his elbows dug into his knees and his baseball cap yanked down over his face. He had already taken the DISC behavioral science assessment, but he had not brought any paperwork or so much as a pen with him. When I walked into the conference room, Jacob didn't acknowledge me in the least, and his body language said it all: "I don't want to be here, and there's no way I'm talking to you about me, my life, or anything else."

Okay then! I cut to the chase and laid out the rules of our engagement:

1) Everything we talk about stays between you and me.

2) If you cannot trust me, I cannot help you.

3) You must own this process. This is your plan and your life, no one else's.

4) If you want, you will communicate with your parents about this process, but I will not.

5) I am here to help you—not your parents—
just you.

6) I can only help if you are open with me. The
more candid and honest you are, the more we
will accomplish.

7) At the end of the process you will choose an
accountability partner to hold you to your plan.

With the rules clear, Jacob's demeanor lightened up
a little, and we began the first of the four steps to the Stop
the Vanilla in Your Career and Life Process.

"So, what do you like to do?" I asked Jacob. A simple
enough question, but it was as if no one had ever asked
him that before. He reacted instantly, straightening right
up in his chair. He wanted to be a chef. He had been working in the kitchen at one of the nicest restaurants in town,
and even though he'd been working on side dishes, he felt
ready for a bigger challenge! As he talked, he took off his
baseball cap and sat up on the edge of his chair.

Now we were getting somewhere. Next, Jacob and I
debriefed his behavioral science results and began talking
about the strength of his high Compliance score. Working with recipes would be a great fit for his high level of
Compliance, and his natural attention to detail would aid
his food presentation ability. Kitchen work is demanding
and can be intense, and as his low Dominance score indicated, he may not want to be an executive chef. Perhaps if
he found the right partner or team to work with, he could
be a tremendous asset—there are plenty of different types
of chefs.

Jacob

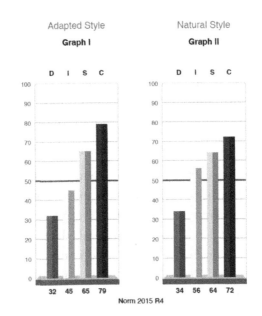

We drew up a few action plans to help him sort through his options. Jacob decided to gain as much diverse experience at his current restaurant as he possibly could. He would work with and shadow line cooks, pastry chefs, even dishwashers. And to keep all his options open, he committed to maintaining average or better grades in his college classes. After much "food" for thought, a different Jacob emerged from the conference room that day.

We scheduled another appointment a month later, to which Jacob brought some extremely positive updates. It was a reminder to me of what a touch of clarity can do for a person's outlook on life! School had been much more tolerable for Jacob now that he had grander plans in mind—his business classes that had previously felt generic and pointless were now personally relevant. He had also been surprised about how much he enjoyed a Spanish class he'd taken on a whim. Meanwhile, Jacob was able to observe and participate in virtually every role at the restaurant where he worked, and he was eager to wrap it all together and finalize his Mint Chocolate Chip Strategy. Together we mapped out Jacob's various life goals (as you will do in Chapter 5) and worked through his choice for an accountability partner (as you'll do in Chapter 6). Jacob was smiling ear-to-ear when he left that day.

A short time later, my wife and I visited the restaurant where Jacob worked. I asked our waiter if Jacob could come and say hello. About ten minutes later, Jacob came out of the kitchen, grubby and greasy from head to toe, but positively beaming. He told us he and a friend were buying a building to start their own restaurant!

What I especially love about Jacob's story is that he simply could not ignore his passion any longer. He showed enough discipline that his parents grew to accept *and encourage* his decision to switch to pursuing a culinary degree. Jacob also stuck with Spanish and is now wholeheartedly pursuing his Mint Chocolate Chip Strategy to partner in a restaurant as a bilingual chef!

Moderate: Matt

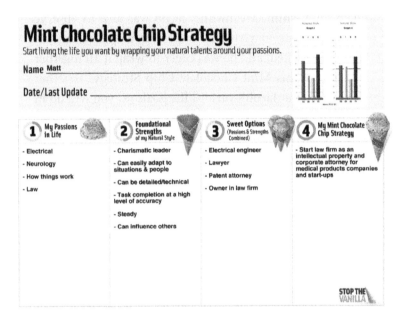

Mint Chocolate Chip Strategy

Start living the life you want by wrapping your natural talents around your passions.

Name Matt

Date/Last Update

1 My Passions in Life
- Electrical
- Neurology
- How things work
- Law

2 Foundational Strengths of my Natural Style
- Charismatic leader
- Can easily adapt to situations & people
- Can be detailed/technical
- Task completion at a high level of accuracy
- Steady
- Can influence others

3 Sweet Options (Passions & Strengths Combined)
- Electrical engineer
- Lawyer
- Patent attorney
- Owner in law firm

4 My Mint Chocolate Chip Strategy
- Start law firm as an intellectual property and corporate attorney for medical products companies and start-ups

STOP THE VANILLA

While the previous examples focused on men and women earlier in their respective careers, it is never, ever too late to love what you do and live the life you want.

Matt was forty-three and running on fumes—not a great way to feel as a sole provider with a wife, two sons, and a mortgage all depending on him. He refused to complain, though, and kept telling himself to tough it out. In spite of Matt's strong self-discipline and work ethic, he was consistently scraping the barrel for energy that seemed to burn up more quickly with each passing week. Even with a loving family at home, Matt was down on life, increasingly disappointed in himself, and worried about the toll his job was taking. Remember Maslow's Hierarchy of Needs in Chapter 1? Matt was losing ground.

Matt's employment as an intellectual property lawyer was leaving him further and further outside that group of passionate 12.3 percent of American workers, especially as more of his company's business was outsourced. Whether from lack of work or lack of passion, Matt was being squeezed out at his firm. But to that point, passion was not even in Matt's vocabulary. He was just concerned with making ends meet to pay his bills and support his family.

Matt had tried working with two different career coaches to little avail. He could not figure out how to package his seemingly incompatible talents. Matt's uncle, Terry, whom I have known a long time, urged Matt to contact me. I was instantly struck by Matt's charisma, impressed by his resume, and excited to help him figure out how to combine his gifts into a lasting, rewarding career.

Talking through his passions, I was surprised to learn that Matt, had always had a passion for electronics, going back to boyhood tinkering with wires and gadgets. He had pursued that passion, going on to earn a degree in electrical engineering, but without formal career planning, he wound up working at a manufacturing company that not only failed to utilize his skills, but also left him questioning his passion altogether.

When his career had not taken off as planned, Matt sought guidance from Terry, who is a tremendously successful lawyer. His Uncle made the case that Matt also had the brains and tenacity to practice law. Encouraged and inspired by the advice, Matt went to law school, specializing in intellectual property protection—a field related to his passion for electronics—because he could support the process of invention. In fairly short order, Matt married, graduated, got a job, bought a house, and brought two energetic little boys into the mix.

Things seemed settled, and for a time, Matt enjoyed his position as an intellectual property attorney for a very large organization. The work was initially interesting to him because it was new and different, but it quickly became routine, and vanilla life set in. Matt still enjoyed some of his leadership responsibilities, but a new boss restructured and effectively took away the team he loved. It had been two years since this happened, and he was somehow managing to fight his near-daily urge to walk out.

After discussing his background and various passions, the two of us started the next step in the Stop the Vanilla in Your Career and Life Process: his DISC behavioral science assessment. As can sometimes be the case, Matt did not have a behavioral style in which he ranked exceptionally high or low in his scores. Rather, his natural behavioral style had more moderate intensity in each of the four DISC factors. His highest, Compliance, was just a hair above his Dominance score, with his Influence score only slightly lower. When this happens, sometimes people feel their results don't completely describe them and the information won't help them. While it can be a little harder to interpret, nothing could be farther from the truth. As a matter of fact, Matt's results epitomized his unique behavioral style. He had a charismatic leadership style, with enough detail orientation to understand

and communicate the technicalities of a product or business, yet the ability to make decisions much faster than the average high Compliance individual. He also adapts to any situation by focusing on the style needed to succeed in the moment. Mixed-bag or not, *all* DISC behavioral science results provide their own unique and equal value.

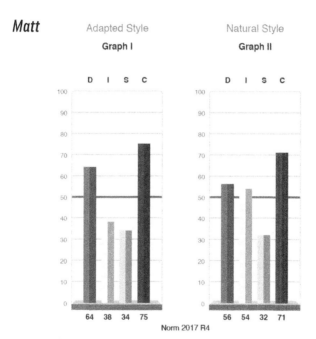

Matt   Adapted Style   Natural Style

Graph I   Graph II

D	I	S	C
64	38	34	75
56	54	32	71

Norm 2017 R4

As we began to discuss the options that might rest at the intersection of Matt's strengths and his passions in life, I asked if any significant life events had ever affected him. He looked at me solemnly and told the story of his wife's brain surgery, fourteen years earlier, for a very serious neurological issue. There was a time, he told me, when it was unclear how she would recover from the surgery. Matt grew emotional and explained that beyond his gratitude for her recovery, he was instilled with a new perspective on life, committing to avoid superficial relationships in favor of deeper connections.

The experience also forced Matt to learn more than he had ever wanted to know about neurological health issues. He never had a passion for biology before, so this new-found interest was surprising to him—until he recognized the parallels between nervous systems and electrical wiring. I'll never forget the conversation because it reminded me that life experiences can be a powerful motivator in someone's life.

Matt's Mint Chocolate Chip Strategy would have to wrap his natural behavioral style around his passions for electronics and neurology, he decided, also while utilizing his legal talents. Once we had defined this intersection, it did not take him long to realize his ideal career: Matt wanted to start his own law firm specializing in intellectual property services for medical device companies and bio-tech start-ups.

After mapping out short-term and long-term objectives, Matt was confident enough to resign from his employer and focus fully on the deeper, more meaningful career that called him.

Creating Your Sweet Options

Now that you've seen examples, it's time for you to start documenting your career options in your Mint Chocolate

Chip Strategy template. (You can do so via the download-able template, or the Stop the Vanilla Career and Life Planning Course at Courses.StopTheVanilla.com.) The Mint Chocolate Chip Strategy template is a tool designed to figure out your optimum career option—the sweetest one of all.

To complete the template:

- In column 1, list the prioritized passions you identified in Chapter 2.

- In column 2, list the strengths of your behavioral style that you identified in Chapter 3.

- In column 3, brainstorm and list as many career options at the intersection of your passions in life and the strengths of your natural behavioral style.

It's important for you to spend some quality time brainstorming as many options as you can before moving on to taste-testing. Recognize as you go through the following taste-testing process that you may discover more career options to add to column 3.

Taste-Testing

Each of the hardworking people above have different life circumstances, behavioral styles, and passions, but what they all have in common is the way they continued to move forward, experiment, brainstorm, and gain clarity. None of them lingered or sat idle. They kept working at it, bringing them ever closer to living a passion and further from misery. They did this by sampling their options until they found the best possible intersection of their passion and natural style. Recognize that this is a journey, not a sprint. All is good, as long as you continue to move forward. We will check in on their progress later in the book.

Since different behavioral styles can be wrapped around a passion in any number of ways, the best way to establish your Mint Chocolate Chip Strategy is to explore your options by engaging in or around them. We call this taste-testing, and recommend utilizing as many of the following techniques as possible to sample the career options you have brainstormed:

- Research online, but by no means rely completely on the internet.

- Meet with people who will ask great questions to expand your thinking.

- Meet with people you know and respect.

- Reach out to different professionals to interview them about their work.

- "Crowd-source" an idea on social media.

- Have lunch with professionals who work in or around the career options you are considering.

- Shadow, intern, take apprenticeships or even side jobs related to your passion.

- Enroll in a class, whether for college credit or not.

- Volunteer and do pro-bono work.

- Seek a position on an advisory board.

- Arrange a gathering of people you know who share your interest.

- Post on a website that reviews independent contractors to gauge interest.

These are just a few suggestions to get the gears between your ears turning—the only real limitation is how widely you want to cast your net. Certainly, do not limit your education here to institutionalized learning. Taste-testing is all about asking around, getting wild ideas, and learning all you can whether that wisdom comes from a college, a colleague, or a mentor.

For career research to yield dynamic results, treat it like the experiment that it is. A non-committal, imaginative, open mind is vital, so try not to talk yourself out of or into anything just yet. In fact, your expectations may be your worst enemy at this point. You will want to engage in different levels of immersion into your research and embrace both spontaneous and calculated trials. Stay as broad in your thinking as you possibly can before you begin to narrow down. Be sure to maintain awareness of any changes in your energy level as you engage and toy with different ideas. What does your conscience, your gut, your "taste buds" tell you? When does the room get brighter for you?

Seek mentors in your network and learn from everyone you can, but ultimately, it's about taste-testing and trying out your options firsthand. As Albert Einstein said, "The only source of knowledge is experience." Appreciate any feedback from those close to you as you go through this stage—make note of it, but do not rely on it. You do not need anyone's permission—just learn as you go!

Double Scoop?

Another benefit to this process of taste-testing is the realization, accumulation, and growth of several different skills. We saw this in Matt's story.

Scott Adams, creator of the long-running, syndicated comic strip, "Dilbert," calls this varied accumulation a "talent stack." Adams' own talent stack would include his exceptional levels of drawing, writing, and business sense.

"When you add in my ordinary business skills, my strong work ethic, my risk tolerance, and my reasonably good sense of humor, I'm fairly unique. And in this case that uniqueness has commercial value," says Adams. He has leveraged his unique talent stack to a net worth nearing nine figures and most importantly, is living the life he wants.

Side Dishes

You start out as broadly as possible, then you begin to narrow down to more specific actions you can take to wrap your natural behavioral style around your passions. As you explore the sweet options you have brainstormed in column 3 of your Mint Chocolate Chip Strategy template, key questions to ask yourself are:

1) Am I passionate about it?

2) Does it come naturally to me?

While this stage is more about learning than earning, the goal is to ultimately identify your best possible career option. These explorations could also lead to a secondary stream of income, a new path after retirement, or simply a new hobby. But foremost, you must meet Maslow's hierarchy of needs from the bottom up, which means you need to see a path to financial security.

If you are planning a career change while you've got significant financial responsibilities, this likely means you'll need to maintain your current job as a source of income while exploring and experimenting during free time. It may require the conjuring of some extra energy. Thankfully, taste-testing and gaining clarity is an energizing process.

You will also gain further clarity, efficiency, and balance as you consider the roles your various passions play in your life. You may learn that a given passion is not something you can monetize, but is better suited as a hobby that adds joy to your life. Take for example Prince, the first-ballot Rock-and-Roll Hall of Fame musician, who never lost his childhood passion for basketball, even though a man only 5'2" tall would likely never make the NBA. Still, the sport helped him clear his head and reset. Wallace Stevens is now famous for his poetry, including "The Emperor of Ice-Cream," but by day, he worked as an executive for an insurance company. Albert Einstein himself claimed to come up with his best ideas in between violin practice sessions.

Hobbies can work wonders for our mental health, giving us a pleasurable point of focus outside of our daily stress. We can certainly be passionate about our hobbies, and that passion and enjoyment can increase when we more clearly define an activity as a pure hobby as opposed to a potential career. I have always loved playing ice hockey, for example, and have only received more enjoyment from the sport since I designated it as a pleasurable hobby. When I was eight years old, I treated rink time like I was headed to the NHL. Finding my Mint Chocolate Chip Strategy elsewhere helped me find peace in recognizing my hockey talent was never enough to put food on the table...let alone buy a table at all.

As I got closer and closer to living my passion for strategy, my income correspondingly increased. Stopping the vanilla in my life did not mean quitting my hobbies. On the contrary, I have had more expendable income and time for hockey than ever before.

Selecting Your Favorite Flavor

While I knew my passion at age twenty-one, I did not learn my natural behavioral style until I was thirty-five. Rather than regret that I did not craft my Mint Chocolate Chip Strategy sooner in life, I'm grateful that I've been able to live my passion ever since. Too many will never know the feeling at all.

When you have determined your career option, write it down in column 4 of the Mint Chocolate Chip Strategy template. If you have not yet chosen your sweet career option, before moving on with the process, continue to gain certainty by experimenting. Try with various combinations of your natural behavioral style and pas-sions in your life until you have crafted the most satisfying recipe you can find. Stick to it—don't stop now.

In the next chapter, you will be making your Mint Chocolate Chip Strategy a reality by plotting out your Rocky Road Life Map.

The Scoop on Next Steps

- In column three of the Mint Chocolate Chip Strategy template, brainstorm and list as many career options at the intersection of your passions in life and the strengths of your natural behavioral style.

- Write your Mint Chocolate Chip Strategy in column four if you have clarity and are ready to move forward. If not, continue taste-testing until you do have clarity.

Your Rocky Road Life Map

"Those Who Plan—PROFIT!"

For more than twenty years, that has been the slogan for our strategy and talent planning consulting firm, Stop the Vanilla, LLC. It's also how I sign off all my columns, blogs, and emails. I want to share the advantage of planning with as many people as possible. It's something of a positive twist on the late Zig Ziglar's famous quote: "If you aim for nothing, you will hit it every time."

People tend to think of profit as monetary, but money is just one component of true wealth. Those who are living at the intersection of their natural behavioral style and their passion understand this firsthand. The time I spend with my family, both the grand and the ordinary moments, is what makes me rich in ways money alone could never provide. For others, profit can mean more time for hiking, mastering new recipes, or rescuing animals. Profit is freedom and having options for enjoying it. Profit means a million things to a million people, but it's a stone-cold truth that we profit more with a plan.

Do you remember ice cream day in grade school? Each student would get a small sealed cup of ice cream and a flat wooden "spoon?" Yes, I can still taste the wood too! The ice cream was always vanilla, wasn't it? No options, just uniform assignment—better than nothing, but still the most boring flavor there is. With apologies to Mr. Ziglar, a personalized version of his quote: If you don't choose your own ice cream, you'll get vanilla every time. Those who choose are rewarded. Those who act deliberately can stop living vanilla.

This is the chapter where you decide how to Stop the Vanilla in Your Career and Life and make your plan to put the bland behind you.

How do you hope to profit from your Mint Chocolate Chip Strategy? We'll be building on the work you've put in so far. Don't worry, you've done much of the heavy lifting already. Now it's time to tie it all together.

Recipe Recap

The previous chapters asked you to define, combine, and refine. By now you've listed your life's passions as well as your natural behavioral strengths, brainstormed career options that see your passions and behavioral style working in concert, and focused on the path that will lead you to rewarding, fulfilling success. I would like to think you are already feeling an initial sense of accomplishment from completing these steps!

Next, we will round up the results of your self-research. You have gained clarity as to who you are and what you want, largely by looking back and pinpointing which topics and activities have historically held your interest. You have begun to realize what you always wanted out of life. You are seeing it all come together: the passions of your past and present and the natural behavioral style that's been with you since childhood.

You've done a lot of reflecting, an undertaking invaluable in and of itself, but the ultimate purpose of understanding and owning who you are is to leverage this knowledge to become the person you want to be. Let's take the life you *have* and turn it into the life you *want*.

The internal analysis you have completed forms the basis of the Stop the Vanilla in Your Career and Life Process. Your next step toward living your passion is to not only stop looking back, but to look further into your future than you ever have before.

A Map to Live the Life You Want

Like most kids, mowing the lawn was not my favorite chore. It did, however, make for an unexpected lesson. No matter how much I concentrated on the mower's wheels in front of me, I would look back at a pass I'd just made in disappointment over how crookedly I'd steered. Of course, my dad wanted his lawn crossed with nice looking, straight lines, so he offered me advice that has stuck with me to this day: Line up, focus my gaze on the endpoint, and push with confidence.

It felt unintuitive, if not vulnerable, to look ahead to the edge of our yard instead of down at the grass and the wheels of the mower. Training myself was tough, but my dad was absolutely right. With his method, my mowing got immediately straighter and the lines became more beautiful. The better it worked, the more I trusted myself to follow through, and vice versa—an upward spiral of improvement and results. When you keep your eyes focused on the end goal, your path will be straight. Sure enough, in mowing the lawn and in life, this is truth!

With a clear endpoint in mind, we are much likelier to take a cleaner and quicker path toward it. The daily minutiae are recognized and minimized, freeing us to look further into the future and focus on our grander life goals. Following a real plan not only leads us to profit in the long term, but also in the short term, by reducing the distractions of minor obstacles and softening the impact of major challenges. "He who has a 'why' to live for can bear almost any 'how,'" said philosopher Friedrich Nietzsche. After the following exercise, you are going to have a clearer "why" to live for than you've ever had, as well as the "how" to get there. We call this personal guide your Rocky Road Life Map.

"He who has a 'why' to live for can bear almost any 'how.'"
—Friedrich Nietzsche

This step in the Stop the Vanilla in Your Career and Life Process is where the rubber meets the road and—ice cream theme aside—the road of life can get rocky. Completing the life map, you will decide upon your destinations, designate the checkpoints, and negate the bumps and detours that could otherwise throw you off course or cancel your trip.

The scenery, however, gets better as you progress. Starting your own business, for example, is a beautiful pit stop. But to see that company grow and prosper to the point of philanthropy and selecting an heir who will carry your dream into the future, well, that is monumental. Whatever your life's goals may be, together they can take you from ordinary to legendary.

I should mention that your Rocky Road Life Map comes with built-in G.P.S. — "Guiding Passion and Style." You'll know you're on the right track as you feel yourself energized and accelerating toward fulfilling your Mint Chocolate Chip Strategy.

Your Rocky Road Life Map plans for three different stages of your life, first by going as far as possible to map out your legacy. That is how you would like to be remembered, the vision for your life, the stamp you impress upon this world, and/or the reasons a monument may one day be erected in your honor. From there, you will work your way back in time, mapping out long-term objectives you will need to achieve en route to fulfilling your legacy. You will then take another step back toward the present and focus on the short-term actions that will start you on this clear path toward true self-actualization, the highest level on Maslow's Hierarchy of Needs.

The template below illustrates the key components of your map—career, personal, and financial—in three stages for each—legacy, long term, and short term—to control the direction of your life. That is the essence of the Rocky Road Life Map. (You can complete the template in the downloadable PDF or the Stop the Vanilla Career and Life Planning Course at Courses.StopTheVanilla.com).

Your career preparation goals can include entrepreneurship, promotions, or completing a college degree or credential of another kind. Your personal goals may cover family, friends, and spirituality. Financially, you may have a mortgage, a car, a debt to pay off, or a hope of something to acquire. Maybe you have the goal of never letting money limit your decisions. Cast your net widely to catch as many of your passions and dreams as possible.

You are officially ready to plot your course, make your Mint Chocolate Chip Strategy a reality, and reap the many rewards that will follow. You have what it takes—are you ready for the adventure?

Zone In

Clarity breeds more clarity—one revelation leads to another. But before you can envision your Rocky Road Life Map, you will need to un-blur your eyes. To wrap your head around a concept as large as the legacy you will leave, you will first need to clear your mind and get into "the zone."

The zone is a temporary, transcendent hot streak of focused brilliance and rhythm. The term is often used for athletes who seemingly cannot miss or fail. Nothing can distract them. You may have watched a professional baseball pitcher's strong start extend into several perfect innings, and noticed his teammates granting him more and more personal space. The players know their pitcher is in his zone, and as much as they would like to cheer him on, they don't want to risk breaking his exceptional concentration.

Great things are accomplished by people who are in the zone—that place in our mind that allows us to perform and think at a higher level. Is there an activity or environment that activates yours? A colleague of mine gets in his zone while listening to the sound of running water. It has such a tremendous effect on his concentration that he has a fountain in his office and another in his home. Another friend of mine gets in her zone while walking. For her, time spent walking is time well spent.

For me, it's bicycling. Whether I am riding outside on my mountain bike or indoors on my stationary bike, pedaling makes my mind produce ideas and solutions I would not have discovered otherwise. I can count on the constant motion, the turning gears, and the increased flow of oxygen to get me into the zone. I even edited my entire first book, *Stop Selling Vanilla Ice Cream*, and this book while riding my stationary bike!

As good as biking has always been for my brain, I still needed to take things to an entirely new level—and location—when I committed to mapping out my life. You will likely also find it beneficial to do your Rocky Road Life Map somewhere comfortable, yet away from your ordinary responsibilities.

I got the idea to plot a one-page plan for my life through a peer group, and it immediately appealed to my passion for strategy. That passion had fueled my consulting company for eight years at that point, and I had helped hundreds of companies significantly increase their profits. Although I made a living creating successful strategy and talent plans for businesses and other people, it dawned on me that I had never created a plan for my own life.

I made this an immediate priority and took it very seriously, even asking a friend if I could borrow his empty cabin an hour north of Green Bay to focus on the process without distractions. Believe me, there was nothing to do but what I came to do. It was the middle of February in Door County, Wisconsin, -2° outside, and for three days, my view was nothing *but nothing*. As far out as I could see, Lake Michigan was frozen. All I had were my writing materials, enough food to last the weekend, and three books to challenge and guide my thinking: *The Bible*, *Rich Dad, Poor Dad* by Robert T. Kiyosaki, and *Halftime* by Bob Buford. (Okay, I also brought two cans of beer, one for each night, to wind down).

You may not need to go to the extent I did to ensure a highly productive environment to work on your Rocky Road Life Map, but because of my behavioral style—namely my tendency to lose interest quickly—I knew I needed to paint myself into a corner mentally, eliminating all potential distractions and leaving myself this one thing to work on. My message to you is to do whatever it takes to tune all the way in.

This begs the question: Why can it be so difficult for us to focus on planning our lives? Why do we have to make it a priority—why isn't it one already? "Brain freeze" might be one way to put it. Not unlike that uncomfortable phenomenon when we eat too much ice cream too quickly, we can overwhelm ourselves by overloading our minds with such grand concepts such as a vision for our career and life. We also get so distracted by life that it's hard to focus on a big-picture strategy. That is why I strongly advocate taking at least a weekend when considering big questions like the following:

1) How do I want to be remembered by my significant other/spouse?

2) How do I want to be remembered by my children?

3) How do I want to be remembered by my parents?

4) How do I want to be remembered by my siblings?

5) How do I want to be remembered by my grandkids?

6) How do I want to be remembered by my friends?

7) How do I want to be remembered by my colleagues/business partners?

8) How do I want to be remembered by my community?

9) How will health, spirituality, and finance impact my legacy?

The answers you have come up with likely span a lot of your priorities and life goals, and that's great! While this book's primary focus is to purposefully link you to the best career possible, it's because meaningful, sustainable, passionate work is the surest means for you to stop living a vanilla life—in aspects well beyond how you earn a living.

Think about older relatives of yours, such as parents or grandparents, whose legacies you respect. What did they do to earn your admiration? Chances are, although you respect their career accomplishments, what you truly admire about these people is their ability to impact others while living on their own terms. What kind of lasting impression will you make on your family members? The Rocky Road Life Map is an excellent tool to consciously consider what uniquely constitutes a successful, respectable, mint-chocolate-chip life for you.

Sticking to Your Map

No one goes from vanilla to Valhalla in a day, though, so you will have two important pit stops along the way. En route to your destination, you will arrange to pull over at a couple of roadside attractions—checkpoints to ensure you're sticking to your map. You'll plot these on your Rocky Road Life Map, working back from your legacy in the right-hand column to your long-term objectives in the center column to your short-term action plans in the left column.

You will feel lighter and pick up speed exponentially once you wave bon voyage to vanilla-ville! These pit stops present opportunities to refuel, reevaluate, appreciate your progress, and tweak your course when needed. They will serve as encouragement and reinforcement that you are heading in the right direction.

This is your exodus to the extraordinary, so I want you to dream as massively as you wish to dream, but not be frustrated when you do not instantly see it all come together. After all, this is a life map, not a day trip!

Long-term objectives and short-term action plans will help you maintain perspective. Let's say one of the goals of your legacy is to become a best-selling fiction writer. Clearly this cannot happen overnight—it'd be like hitting 100 miles an hour the moment your toe brushed the gas pedal. With such an ambitious legacy goal in mind, your long-term objective may be to sell two thousand books by your fortieth birthday, and your short-term action plan may be to get the book outline and first chapter written in three months.

If another goal for your legacy is to pay for your grandchildren's college education, your long-term objective may be to pay for your children's education, and your short-term action plan may be to set up an educational savings plan with a serious commitment to aggressively funding the account.

Or, if a goal for your legacy is to spend time in ten different countries, you may set the long-term objective of visiting five by the time you are fifty, and the short-term action plan of visiting two of them by your thirty-fifth birthday.

Measurability is Key

Whether you are aiming for a certain quantity or assigning a deadline to a specific action plan, setting your aim at something ill-defined or abstract will prevent you from making or knowing when you've made real progress.

You have innumerable possibilities here, and writing yours out in these three stages of goals is an act meant to free your potential and point you toward living your passion. The Rocky Road Life Map is a helpful trail, not a trap—a source of guiding inspiration, not incarceration. It's a living document for your life, requiring at least an annual review, which we'll work through later in the book.

Sample Scoops

As the creator of the Stop the Vanilla in Your Career and Life Process, I unknowingly worked toward forging my Mint Chocolate Chip Strategy long before I'd named any of the steps, shared it with others, or even recognized it as a process at all. While my life did improve after wrapping my natural style around my passion, if I hadn't created my Rocky Road Life Map, I would never have written my first book, let alone this one, nor would I have given speeches all over the world. These accomplishments are not to boast, but rather prove that when you are passionate about what you do and deliver it naturally, you will get rewarded for it.

Before you begin your own map, you may find it helpful to view portions of mine, as well as Jacob's and Brittany's, who you met earlier.

Rocky Road Life Map

Name Steve

Date/Last Update

	Short-Term Action Plans Actions to achieve my long-term objectives and legacy	Due Date	Long-Term Objectives By 12/31/2030 Objectives to achieve my legacy	My Legacy How I want to be remembered
Personal	Date night every Wednesday		Develop plan with my wife to define our vision together. Marriage retreats.	My wife knows she is first in my life
	Set annual vacation		Travel to see my kids often, and review their career/life plan consistently	Kids are successful, have great families, and view me as a mentor/adult friend
	Workout 4x a week		Maintain a healthy lifestyle, always feel comfortable. No gut! Live to the age of 85	Live a long and healthy life
Professional	Develop annual strategy and talent plan for company		Establish Board of Advisors	Stop The Vanilla, LLC is widely known, respected, and positively impacts many lives
	Update my volunteer plan—where my skills bring the greatest value		Define key causes to support	Impact lives through my passions and gifts
Financial	Develop financial plan with advisor and accountant		Pay off all debt except house	Don't let cost decide what we choose to experience
	Implement new family budget		Build emergency fund	No arguments with my wife about money issues

STOP THE VANILLA

My Mint Chocolate Chip Strategy: Strategy and Talent Thought Leader/Advisor/Speaker/Author

Rocky Road Life Map

Name **Jacob**   Date/Last Update _____

Short-Term Action Plans Actions to achieve my long-term objectives and legacy	Due Date	Long-Term Objectives By 12/31/2035 Objectives to achieve my legacy	My Legacy How I want to be remembered
Personal			
Go to annual Packer game with my dad		Make all family holiday get-togethers	Connected relationships with family/parents
Professional			
Get culinary degree		Bilingual chef	Respected chef and restaurateur
Get knowledge of farming/responsible sourcing		Operator/Owner of a restaurant	Provide memorable food experience
			Educate customer on origin and sustainability of food source
Financial			
Start saving for down payment on building		Profitable restaurant(s)	Financially independent

My Mint Chocolate Chip Strategy: **Chef and Restaurateur**

STOP THE VANILLA

Rocky Road Life Map

Name ___Brittany___   Date/Last Update _____

	Short-Term Action Plans Actions to achieve my long-term objectives and legacy	Due Date	Long-Term Objectives By 12/31/2035 Objectives to achieve my legacy	My Legacy How I want to be remembered
Personal	Touch base with each sibling monthly		Meet annually with siblings	Have connected relationships with my siblings
Professional	Complete residency		Research options to improve total patient health	Care for total health of patients, especially those with chronic illnesses
			Complete pediatric oncology fellowship	
Financial	Develop financial plan with advisor		Pay off student loans	Little to no financial pressure/financially secure
	Develop annual budget			

My Mint Chocolate Chip Strategy: **Pediatric Oncologist and Public Health**

STOP THE VANILLA

Seize the Momentum!

Your turn! Now that you have studied three abbreviated examples, it is your turn to complete your own Rocky Road Life Map! I am excited for you or anyone who does this—possibly even more excited than you are for yourself. Try to savor the process, especially if you have never done anything like this before, and tune into any breakthroughs that you experience. Does the clarity make you perk up a bit? As with the rest of the Stop the Vanilla in Your Career and Life Process, your positive reactions are clues that you are getting closer to your sweet spot. Seize that momentum and keep going!

To reiterate, you will start with your end game (right column) and work your way to the present (left column). A destination gives you direction and urgency, focuses your decisions on what is important, minimizes distractions, and maximizes your limited time and resources.

Your legacy in the right column asks the biggest questions. How do you want to be known? What does it look like to you to personally excel? Some find it beneficial to view the legacy as writing your own best-case epitaph: "I would like to be remembered as a _____ person." Others will consider concerns about how they are viewed externally, and productively channel their aspirations to be objectively admired: "I have always wanted to be seen as a _____ person." Another technique is to simply visualize a life that would be uniquely enjoyable and thinking more in terms of vision rather than legacy: "The vision for my life is _____."

For the middle column, choose how far out you want to set the point for your long-term objectives—typically ten or twenty years out works well. Just make sure you are working with a measurable deadline and record it in your Rocky Road Life Map template. A real, attainable time in the future that you can measure is usually better than an abstraction like "the midpoint of my career" or "after I retire."

Lastly, that left column is where you really start to stop living vanilla. This is the present, the now, the time for you to build whatever you want with what you already have. It's a time to define and complete specific action plans that take the first step toward achieving your long-term objectives and legacy. It is essential that you add a due date to each action plan to ensure you are held accountable to complete them. Later, we will cover the process for reviewing and updating your overall map and the other columns. But there is no need to wait on editing items in the left column, as long as you're actively working toward making your right column a reality.

Those who are earlier in their career may find more value in the short-term action plans that lead to achieving the long-term objectives, while those later in their career may find more value in defining and working toward their legacy. But whatever your age, the Rocky Road Life Map makes your vision a reality.

Always Take Steps Forward

The bottom line is when you make moves, you continue to get clarity. Always be taking steps forward, even if it means occasional shortcomings. A Japanese proverb says, "Vision without action is a daydream. Action without vision is a nightmare." Vision *with* action is your Rocky Road Life Map!

> *Vision with action is your Rocky Road Life Map!*

The Scoop on Next Steps

Complete the first draft of your Rocky Road Life Map.

6

Fire Up the Ice Cream Truck

"Every great athlete, artist, and aspiring being has a great team to help them flourish and succeed—personally and professionally. Even the so-called 'solo star' has a strong supporting cast helping them shine, thrive, and take flight."

—Rasheed Ogunlaru

ehind every successful person is a multitude of allies. The Stop the Vanilla in Your Career and Life Process is an individualized exercise of self-improvement and transformation. While it's ultimately up to you to follow through with your Rocky Road Life Map, you shouldn't have to go it alone.

You have invested incredible effort on your own so far, and you are the primary power for seeing this process through, but it's time to call for backup. I highly recommend enlisting at least one co-pilot to help navigate this bold route you have plotted for your life—a partner who is there for you along the way as you execute the impressive plan you've created.

Don't Go It Alone!

We call this compatriot your accountability partner, but you may call yours what you will, so long as you call him or her regularly. This is the person who, per your request, will be committed to keep you on course to make your legacy become reality. He or she needs to have permission to call you out if you begin to drift back to the status quo of drudgery. I suggest you plan monthly conversations together, but you can talk more if needed. Your meetings should be candid, caring, and collaborative, for this is a symbiotic agreement in which you will both support, and if necessary, challenge one another.

I have to admit, the concept of an accountability partner snuck up on me. Even after I had been humbled by learning about my natural behavioral style at age thirty-five, I never would have thought I needed anyone but myself to stick to my life map. I have never been one to ask for help—or directions for that matter!

A few years back, I met two entrepreneurs at a consulting conference. Brent Patmos, Ryan Lisk, and I hit it off immediately. We were like brothers from other mothers who had been scattered across the country. All three of us were close in age, going through similar stages in our lives, and in approximately the same progression of building our own companies. With so much in common, we quickly established a strong and honest camaraderie.

In sharing our current situations in life as well as our career goals, Brent, Ryan, and I realized we could learn a lot from each other and agreed it could be advantageous for us all to stay in contact and reconnect regularly. It was a mastermind group of sorts.

Our partnership proved to be as productive as we all had hoped. In the ensuing years of phone calls, video chats, meeting up at conferences, and road tripping to each other's towns, the three of us made far more financial, professional, and personal progress than we ever would have if we'd bullishly chosen to go it alone. Achievement can be contagious! All three of us have now published books and built successful consulting firms that positively impact the lives of leaders and their teams. I cannot overstate the positive impact of being held accountable by someone you respect—who wants you to succeed and who can walk a mile in your shoes.

Does anyone come to mind as a good candidate for you? Having another person to hold you accountable will keep your personal goals more firmly in the forefront of your mind than if you try to create your own system of checks and balances.

On our own, we can easily justify missteps and failures. Unsupervised, we can get distracted and carelessly lose the plot, even when the plot is our own creation. Without our peers' constructive counsel, it's much more likely that a Rocky Road Life Map will go by the wayside even if we work very hard at it. As important as it is to stop living vanilla and to start living your passion, an accountability partner will be there to ensure you *continue* doing so. You need the map and the partnership because smooth traveling is far from guaranteed.

Your accountability partner will be there to celebrate your progress, put the setbacks into perspective, help you rev up for challenges on the horizon, and keep you on the right course in spite of obstacles. Your accountability partner is there to advise you, encourage you, and simply listen when you need to vent.

Return the Favor

While some partnerships see only one person holding the other accountable, I suggest trying to find a partner who wants the same help from you. Ideally, you will fuel each other's drive and determination to succeed. Any good co-pilot would share your desire to move forward and improve. The more you have in common, the better. It's unlikely you'll find someone whose lot in life is identical to your own, but at a minimum your accountability partner should:

- Share the same values.

- Be someone you trust.

- Be reliably accessible and easy to contact.

- Respond within a few hours of critical requests.

- Be willing to deliver tough love and accountability, but also understand when you simply need support and compassion.

- Have walked in your shoes, had similar life circumstances, and/or the ability to relate to your situation.

To expand on that last item, it is not required, but helpful if you and your accountability partner are going through similar stages or seasons in your lives and careers. Such correlation makes for deeper connection and empathy, and you will feel like you are helping yourselves by helping each other, while facing many of the same challenges. My accountability partners and I overcame many obstacles by talking through them until someone recognized a problem from his own experience, and applied the solution to the current challenge. This builds the collaborative sense that no hurdle is too high for your accountability partner and you.

When you have someone suitable in mind, the process for striking a partnership could go as follows:

1) Meet in person. The initial discussion should be face-to-face, in step with the personal nature of what will be ongoing and open dialogue.

2) Share the concept. He or she may not be familiar with accountability partnerships, so make sure to communicate the idea and your desire to be held accountable, as well as requirements and expectations. You'll need to ask him or her directly to play this important role and give them time to think about it.

3) Go for it! In each other you have found a reliable advisor who will provide your Mint Chocolate Chip Strategy checkup. He or she does not necessarily need to be familiar with the Stop the Vanilla in Your Career and Life Process, though going through it with each other provides a great foundation for accountability and success.

Anecdotally, the most successful people I have met have a trusted comrade they consistently chat with over coffee, lunch, a Friday afternoon margarita, or even an ice cream sundae.

A Spoonful of Sugar

We receive constructive criticism from our family and close friends because we know they care about us. Your accountability partner may not be someone especially close to you, but in order for you to willingly take his or her advice to heart, you'll need to find someone you fully trust, who wants you to become all that you aspire to be.

To establish a healthy and open exchange of ideas—especially the difficult ones—you and your partner need to agree on some rules of engagement which should include:

- Confidentiality (everything stays between accountability partners)
- No judgment
- Transparency

- Vulnerability (willingness to be open and unguarded)
- Reciprocity (recognition that this is a two-way street)
- Established objectives and measurements
- Mutual agreement
- Consistency in contact and check-ins
- Professionalism and respect
- Action plans (your Rocky Road Life Map)

Finding the right partnership is about maximizing the accountability to the Rocky Road Life Map you have plotted, by way of healthy, productive, and honest conversations. But partnerships are also about celebrating successes and the genuine peace of knowing that regardless of what happens, you've got someone to help you work through it.

Picking Your Partner

Scan your contacts for potential candidates to be your accountability partner, such as:

- Best friend
- Board member
- Advisor
- Counselor
- Sibling
- Peer in your industry

- Spouse*
- Colleague*

I have asterisked the last two suggestions as matters of caution: Designating a person too adjacent to your daily life can limit the gainful objectivity of an accountability partnership. In other words, someone *in* your life may not be able to help you work *on* your life. An accountability partner plays a distinct role in your life: The person you can talk to about anything and everything. While a spouse or colleague may seem like your best option, choosing one will eventually limit the scope of your discussions, if not run the risk of souring rapport and breeding negativity at work or home. To make for maximum transparency on all of the topics the two of you wish to address, I recommend someone more removed from your conflicts and struggles, someone who is less directly affected by your decisions.

A further point of consideration is familiarity. A good accountability partner may be a close friend with great understanding of your past and present; someone you have any established chemistry with who enables you to speak freely. Or, as was the case for Brent, Ryan, and me, a relative stranger who works in your industry can make for a less biased, more equitable voice of reason and guidance. You won't harbor any worries about discussing mutual acquaintances, and assuming you are geographically distant, you won't be in direct competition, making discussion of specifics such as financial information more comfortable. Your Rocky Road Life Map is meant to encompass all professional, financial, and personal aspects of your life—so you need to be able to talk in detail about these life topics with your accountability partner. If a partner is a close co-worker, for example, one can foresee a lack of candor when discussing a current work situation—a topic that requires real conversational freedom. Some of the most valuable advice will come from an external, impartial third party, so use discretion. On the spectrum ranging from best friend to total stranger, strike the balance wherever the conversations will flow easiest.

The perfect accountability partner may be an obvious choice or a surprising one. Ultimately, the person/people you choose is/are a support system for you. **Do not forego an accountability partner just because you cannot find the perfect candidate.** You likely will not be choosing anyone permanently. They should be someone going through struggles or adventures roughly parallel to your own, but it is completely natural and likely your paths will diverge over time. Part of the transparency required of a successful accountability partnership is a candid acknowledgement of whether the partnership is still bringing value to all involved.

Sticking Together

Despite the initial rush of developing a plan for one's life, the toughest time to be accountable to a Rocky Road Life Map is early on, during the short-term action stage. You will feel a sense of self-perpetuating momentum as you get closer to delivering your passion naturally and investing in making your desired legacy a reality. However, as you grow accustomed to this new momentum, the thrill of its newness will naturally fade, and you may lose sight of your vision. This happens all the time with people who take up weightlifting for the first time. They will feel incredibly excited at the novelty of their new training regimen and be enamored by the earliest results when they've got the most room for improvement. As they settle into a routine and their gains are more subtle, many lose their sense of drive and abandon the effort altogether. I often must remind myself, that this is a marathon, not a sprint.

The first steps are often the shakiest, and an accountability partner will help you focus on your endpoint and stay sturdy, the way looking toward land can help keep someone from feeling seasick. You will know you've chosen a quality accountability partner by the progress you make. Encouragement is at the heart of the partnership, but he or she must be much more than a cheerleader. Sometimes accountability hurts—it's not always fun to have someone burst our bubble. But when we need it, we really do need it! If one partner begins to consistently underachieve, the other's got to call him or her out honestly and respectfully.

Other times, you will call your partner just to get something off your chest—no judgment or suggestions solicited, no damage done; simply a technique to level out. "How are you holding up?" is a common, open-ended question in these discussions—perfect for kicking off a meaningful chat.

These interactions are about optimizing each other's success. It's often helpful to agree on a thirty-minute conversation to discuss whatever he or she wants. In that amount of time, you can stay focused on one's current top challenge or opportunity to develop a plan to succeed in the situation. So favorable was the cooperation and so healthy was the trust between my accountability partners and me that we'd even share our companies' annual business plans with each other, not just for feedback and constructive criticism, but also to consolidate our collective wisdom for the others' benefit. This openness and awareness served to improve our individual plans, as well as our ability to hold each other accountable.

In a competitive market it can be a huge advantage— and just plain refreshing—to have an accountability partner by effectively pooling resources together to compete against the rest of the world. The breakthroughs you experience individually and as a group are transformational. Besides, success is just more fun when you get to celebrate it with others who appreciate the context and the effort of your achievements. To continue that success, your accountability partner will help you stick to your Rocky Road Life Map, and also alert you to points that merit revision and review—the focus of the next chapter.

The Scoop on Next Steps

Select an accountability partner.

7

The Next Scoop

"The first time you make something, follow the recipe, then figure out how to tailor it to your own tastes."

—Ruth Reichl

Reichl's passion—food—led her to a Mint Chocolate Chip Strategy of being a food critic. Her writing has been as popular as it is prestigious, garnering four James Beard awards for excellence in culinary writing. While Reichl's quote above refers to a literal recipe, it applies just as well to your next step: revising and updating your Rocky Road Life Map.

In spite of all her success, Reichl would see the need to revise her strategy and tailor it to keep up with her changing tastes and evolving priorities, especially after the birth of her first child. Years of observing meals led her to appreciate the value of family dinners, and she suddenly found herself desiring more time at home with her husband and new son. This did not mean she had abandoned her prior passion, rather she had added a significant priority to her life. For Reichl, it meant a new dimension to her strategy—instead of constantly traveling to attend and critique restaurants, she would shift to less frequent, yet more prominent appearances on food-related television and radio shows. Her accolades had afforded her the ability to become more selective, while continuing to raise her profile as a food critic.

Although you have made the bold decision to definitively quit living a lackluster life, the process carries forward much longer than that single moment. It is ongoing and continually begs your engagement and commitment. Consciously checking in on and mindfully appreciating the progress you have made on your Mint Chocolate Chip Strategy is akin to a sugar rush without the crash. Further—as was the case with Reichl—active reassessment of your priorities and values, as well as a regular review of your Rocky Road Life Map will ensure you are always accounting for what's important in your life. Changes in your nuclear family, expanding your worldview, or adapting to new opportunities related to your income or health can affect your plan. A bump in the road doesn't mean you've failed. It means you are human, and your map has allowances for it.

You have a duty to yourself, your happiness, and those you care about to allow for these changes in your Rocky Road Life Map. You will only gain clarity and get better at this process the more you do it, so don't worry.

Tweaking the Recipe

Reviewing your Rocky Road Life Map is not about change for the sake of change, nor trying to fix what is not broken. If you have been hitting your stride, meeting your deadlines, and feeling as much enthusiasm and momentum as you ever have, then stick close to your path!

While it's important to have faith in your destination in spite of any potholes or detours you may hit, regularly reassessing your map is a must. At the very least, you will reaffirm your goals and renew your vigor to live your passion; avoiding a relapse or a reversal to your vanilla past. Happiness is hard work—there is no single, permanent way to achieve it, and the only thing tougher than finding happiness is sustaining it.

To do so, it's not uncommon for at least some adjustments to arise. While your natural behavioral style is largely locked in by now, your goals and passions can expand, contract, change directions, or even surprise you! What worked best for me was to update my Rocky Road Life Map every 6 months for the first couple years. Now I update it once a year the second weekend of January, when I can employ last year's knowledge and numbers to reset, reenergize, and reengage. You might choose to complete this the first day of spring and/or fall each year or the first weekend after your birthday. Whenever you find it most effective, scheduling a regular review will ensure that your plan becomes a reality. Regardless, your Rocky Road Life Map merits a thorough review at least every year.

Treat this like a necessary, guided, mental hygiene checkup (if not the full-on spiritual scan) that it is. The review can be completed in a day, an incredibly low investment of time considering the high-level of strategizing involved to create it. The large results it yields over the next year are worth it! As you did when you first plotted your course, you will want to get yourself to a silent place for some uninterrupted mind and soul searching as you consider the following questions to update your Rocky Road Life Map:

1) Where are you at in carrying out your plan? First, give yourself proper credit on the progress you have made. Further, how have you felt? How have those around you—especially your accountability partner(s)—felt about this new, non-vanilla you?

2) Is your Mint Chocolate Chip Strategy working? Feeling good is one thing, but are you getting results? Are you excelling naturally and being rewarded for it? Are you loving what you do? Have you recently discovered new passions? Your behavioral style will not change, but your passions certainly can change. If you are not enjoying some aspect of your current career path, consider re-evaluating your Mint Chocolate Chip Strategy to define what your options are. Should you revisit the taste-testing phase? Do you need to spend some time with your accountability partner?

3) Are you moving toward your long-term objectives and legacy? As you have grown as a person, do you have new goals? Family, finance, spiritual, or any other types of personal priorities may have revealed themselves to you since you last mapped. This is the time to update your legacy and long-term objectives and then add new action plans and due dates to take another step toward achieving them.

4) Action plans. How are you doing on your deadlines? If you have breezed by them, does that change your path? If you have fallen short or behind, was it because life threw you a roadblock or because a certain goal is not as important as you thought it was? Or was a due date simply overambitious and unrealistic?

This process is about crafting a recipe, not a magic spell. Seize the opportunity to consistently revisit your Rocky Road Life Map to make sure you live the life you want. For the items on your Rocky Road Life Map that are not so easily measurable or quantifiable, use your due dates as your metrics. Be honest with yourself about why some goals may have gone unmet.

Are there days when the struggle is less than exciting? Of course. There will be highs and lows of both energy and productivity, but are you moving forward and gaining clarity? You'll get a greater grasp on your progress by reviewing your Rocky Road Life Map right to left—the same order as when you designed it—starting with the items in your legacy column, then your long-term objectives, and finally your short-term action plans.

Reviewing Your Legacy

We all tend to think our plans are going to whimsically change, but when you're dealing with something as grand as your life's legacy, the changes will be incremental at most. You will find yourself tweaking that column less and less with time. Still, there is incredible affirmation and direction as your legacy column solidifies—this always makes for new energy. If there are any changes, it is critical to implement them during the review.

Reviewing Long-Term Objectives

Your long-term column will be subject to a bit more change and scrutiny. In fact, more clarity on your legacy column will lead you to make necessary edits to your more immediate objectives as well. As you know, they are interconnected. You cannot get from A to C if you don't know how to get to B. Each year, you should get more clarity on your long-term objectives and be able to fine-tune them, or even add a couple of objectives based on life changes.

Reviewing Short-Term Action Items

Your short-term column is where editing is likely, and is the reason why reviewing your Rocky Road Life Map every six to twelve months for the first few years can be a very good idea. Ideally you have completed your action plans and are ready for a new set to take another step toward your long-term objectives and legacy.

However, you'll likely find that some action items need to be repeated. For example, part of my legacy is to have connected relationships with my three brothers, so planning a brothers' weekend is in my action plans every year. That's how important it is to me. The key question here: What action plans are you going to complete in the next year (or six months) to get you closer to your legacy? Once your action plans are finalized, add a due date to each action plan.

Sticking It Out

These reviews are about resisting natural regression, fighting a drift back to default, and ensuring you never stop resisting the vanilla. Maintaining your hard-earned momentum will prevent distractions, delays, and derailment from your Rocky Road Life Map. Setbacks do occur, but focusing on your life's vision enables you to take them in stride. Keep your eye on the compass, affirm and reaffirm your life's goals, and consciously congratulate yourself on how much closer you are to living your passion than you've ever been before. As Bon Scott from the rock band AC/DC would put it: "Ride on!"

As you will see in the final chapter, your perseverance has only begun to reward you, but the progress is more than exciting! Don't you already feel more confident as you take your next steps? You are heading toward a good year, a great decade, and an outstanding life!

The Scoop on Next Steps

Review and update your Mint Chocolate Chip Strategy and Rocky Road Life Map on a consistent basis (every six or twelve months).

8

Just Desserts

"If you're not reaching back to help anyone,
then you're not building a legacy."

—Germany Kent

Becoming a Shepherd of Talent

I trust that the four-step process in this book has, and will work wonders for your career and life, the way that it has for so many others. Share your breakthrough of self-improvement with those around you—they will benefit too. Seeing the results of the Stop the Vanilla in Your Career and Life Process in my clients, family, and friends has been as rewarding as it was for me to experience the process in my own life. Some of the greatest growth you will experience as a leader will come from helping others grow.

Once you're loving what you do and living the life you want, I believe it is your solemn duty to shepherd the talent in those around you: your children, siblings, friends, nieces, nephews, and anyone else you know whose life should be anything but vanilla. A shepherd nurtures, cares for, develops, and holds accountable the talent they are responsible for. Every organization (and every home) needs a shepherd of the talent, and now, that can be you!

Business leaders, once you have figured out your Mint Chocolate Chip Strategy, then shepherd the talents of your direct reports. Do it not just because it's the right thing to do, but because your organization will immediately benefit. You will have team members in each position who are passionate about what they do, leading to a high-performance team and company.

If your employees know that you want them to love what they do, *even if it means doing it in a different organization*, they will run through walls for you. Your company will build an employer-of-choice culture.

Focusing on life's passions, utilizing behavioral science to understand, own, and leverage your natural behavioral style, exploring the options at the intersection of passion and style, and mapping out a plan to encompass all aspects of life is an amazing place to be. You and those around you will be looking at those vanilla days in the rearview mirror. The Stop the Vanilla in Your Career and Life Process yields incredible personal breakthroughs. I promised some updates on the people whose stories you have heard. They embody all the potential of stopping the vanilla. Some have just begun the process and exemplify the early successes that can come in this life-changing process.

High Dominance: Aaron

Aaron's Mint Chocolate Chip Strategy of selling life-saving cardiovascular products has been a limitless success. He is honoring his late father by helping provide incredibly advanced technology that will spare others from health issues and tragic losses. Aaron married recently, and he and his wife Kelly are expecting their first child. A recent ultrasound informed them it's a boy! Aaron has always been driven by his desire for financial security, and the Stop the Vanilla in Your Career and Life Process has put him in a position to earn more than ever, just in time for his growing responsibilities as a first-time father.

High Influence: Brittany

Britt—that is, *Dr. Brittany,* has graduated from medical school. Her Mint Chocolate Chip Strategy of pediatric oncology has taken her to the next big step: becoming a resident physician at one of the top pediatric residency programs in the country. What a memory it was for the two of us, father and daughter, as we drove the moving truck to her new destination. She is getting so much closer to achieving the long-term objective she made eight years ago.

Britt is our oldest child, and the furthest along on the Rocky Road Life Map she created when she was still in her teens. My wife and I have witnessed all four of our kids become more independent, confident, and successful as they have taken charge of their lives and careers. The impact of the process has been priceless not only for

Brittany, but for her dear old dad, as nothing is more gratifying than seeing your kids live the life they want.

High Steadiness: Mackenzie

Mackenzie continues to execute her Mint Chocolate Chip Strategy of family therapy with the guidance of her Rocky Road Life Map. Since graduating with her Master's in Marriage and Family Therapy, she passed her licensing exam and is building a family and children's therapy practice within a counseling organization. As a therapist, Mackenzie is working in a career that is a natural fit for her, while improving the lives of hundreds of children and their families—and at the same time enriching her own life.

High Compliance: Jacob

Jacob continues to pursue his Mint Chocolate Chip Strategy of opening his own restaurant, and has made the considerable jump to a prestigious culinary school in California. Once upon a time, his parents may have written-off this move as reckless and irresponsible, but as a result of the work he's put into his Rocky Road Life Map and the progress he's made so far, all the trust in their relationship has been restored. Jacob's parents now fully encourage his career choice, aided by consistent and healthy communication between them. His folks were so worried, and candidly, I was worried too. However, through the Stop the Vanilla in Your Career and Life Process, Jacob has persevered and is on his way to loving what he does for a living in order to live the life he wants!

Moderate: Matt

After taste-testing several options, Matt decided to hang his shingle and start his own law firm specializing in intellectual property and commercial legal work for medical device companies and bio-tech start-ups, and it's going very well! While that may sound like a mouthful, it's because of how specific Matt was able to be when formulating his Mint Chocolate Chip Strategy. *Stop the Vanilla in Your Career and Life* has become part of his professional story, as it can for anyone.

"I cannot think of a time when I was as energized and excited about the future," Matt recently wrote to me, sharing that he's got plenty of clients already. What an update from a forty-three-year-old sole provider for his family—a turnaround he would not have dared predict when he was stuck back at his old job. "Thanks for pushing as you did on the passion piece," he concluded.

Matt's motivation has always centered on controlling his own future, which can easily feel beyond our control when we have others depending on us. Behavioral science helped Matt understand, own, and leverage his entrepreneurial proclivities, such as fast intuition and willingness to take reasonable risk. He credits his firm's competitive advantage to his commitment to this process and feels he is right where he belongs: in the driver's seat and revving forward on his Rocky Road Life Map.

Final Scoop

Like the examples above, I want to congratulate you on your hard work and progress. Perhaps you've worked through all four steps and are excited for the changes to come. Maybe some of you read the book through, cover to cover, and now want to engage with the Stop the Vanilla in Your Career and Life Process. I want to commend you for being resilient and for wanting to improve your quality of life and happiness. Welcome to the minority group of America's workforce that has knowledge of their passions and behavioral style–those who love what they do, deliver it naturally, and get rewarded for it. They are people living a passion, not just having a job. Once you join this select group, you will never leave.

There is no doubt you have increased the clarity of your career and life, and learned how to help others do the same. Remember, greater clarity is always in front of you—not beside or behind you—so keep pursuing the life you want.

The Stop the Vanilla Team is here to help you achieve the vision for your business, career, and life with the right strategy and right talent. We encourage you to visit StopTheVanilla.com for helpful content including the weekly Scoop newsletter, podcast, videos, templates, and links to our social media.

Our Mint Chocolate Chip is helping you define yours, so we would love for you to join our private Facebook Group to work through your challenges, share your successes, and so we can all learn from each other. You can join the Facebook Group by going to Facebook.com/groups/stvcareerandlife. I can't wait to hear your success stories, as you love what you do to live the life you want!

Summary of Steps to Develop Your Career and Life Plan

Chapter 1

1. Options for you to you complete the process as you go through the book are as follows:

    a. Download the PDFs of the Passions Worksheet, Mint Chocolate Chip Strategy and Rocky Road Life Map templates at StopTheVanilla.com/Resources.

    b. Subscribe to the Stop the Vanilla Career and Life Planning Course to guide you through the process at Courses.StopTheVanilla.com.

Chapter 2

1. In the Passions Worksheet:

    a. Brainstorm and list all your passions in the second column.

    b. Rank your passions starting with your greatest passion as number 1, etc., in the first column.

    c. Enter a star next to all the items you enjoy and could get paid to do in the third column.

2. Enter your final passions from the Passions Worksheet into the first column in the downloadable Mint Chocolate Chip Strategy PDF, or in the Stop the Vanilla Career and Life Planning Course at Courses.StopTheVanilla.com.

Chapter 3

1. Contact us at Info@StopTheVanilla.com to purchase a DISC behavioral science assessment.

2. Using your assessment results and life experiences, enter your greatest strengths into the second column in the downloadable Mint Chocolate Chip Strategy PDF, or in the Stop the Vanilla Career and Life Planning Course at Courses.StopTheVanilla.com.

Chapter 4

1. Brainstorm and list as many career options at the intersection of your passions in life and the strengths of your natural behavioral style, and enter them in column 3 of the Mint Chocolate Chip Strategy PDF, or in the Stop the Vanilla Career and Life Planning Course at Courses.StopTheVanilla.com.

2. Write your Mint Chocolate Chip Strategy in column four if you have clarity and are ready to move forward. If not, continue taste-testing until you do have clarity.

Chapter 5

1. Complete the first draft of your Rocky Road Life Map.

   a. Consider the questions on page 103 and complete column three.

   b. Determine your long-term objectives and a date to achieve them, and enter in column two.

   c. In column one, list your short-term action plans with due dates for each to achieve your long-term objectives and legacy.

Chapter 6

1. Select an accountability partner

Chapter 7

1. Review and update your Mint Chocolate Chip Strategy and Rocky Road Life Map on a consistent basis (every six or 12 months)

Acknowledgements

To our clients, thank you for your passion, inspiration, and trust in Stop The Vanilla, LLC. Watching you achieve success is my greatest motivation and professional reward.

My foundation is my faith and family. Thank you to my parents Don and Mary Jane for building a tight knit family that includes my sisters Mary and Diane, and my brothers Paul, Dave, and Andy.

To my board of advisors who have been with me from the start. I want to thank Mark Kaiser, Tim Kneeland, and Dana Vanden Heuvel for challenging, guiding, and encouraging me

Matt Day, you are a brilliant writer whose Mint Chocolate Chip Strategy will become a reality. Your passion and commitment to create a book that is a great read kept me going.

To our Stop The Vanilla Team who helps make my crazy ideas happen. Thank you, Cindy, for your unwavering dedication and support of me and Stop The Vanilla. To Jordan, thank you for your unquenchable desire to learn and challenging me/us to try new ideas and keep getting better. Mark, thank you for always being there as a great sounding board and a true friend.

To my four kids Brittany, Mitchel, Brooke, and Mackenzie: Your work ethic to excel in your chosen career paths and lives inspires me, and watching your success is one of my greatest rewards. I love each of you dearly.

Lisa, you have supported me for 30+ years, have made many sacrifices for our family and enabled me to pursue my Mint Chocolate Chip Strategy. Can't wait to spend the next 30 years with you, my best friend. All my love to you.

And to Walter our wiener dog, thanks for always being able to make me laugh.

Get the Companion Career and Life Planning Course

If being guided through the career and life planning process will help you love what you do for a living, have author Steve Van Remortel be your video guide through the **Stop the Vanilla in Your Career and Life Online Course.**

What's in the Course?

- Steve walks through each step of the process to love what you do for a living to live the life you want.

- This online course includes all you need to complete the process including an eBook, behavioral science assessment, templates, and videos on how to complete each step.

- The course includes short and focused videos to complete each step of the process.

- The course includes a bonus module on how to become a Shepherd of the Talent to help others love what they do for a living and live the life they want.

"Without passion your natural style is not focused, without your natural style your passion is not enjoyed"

—Steve Van Remortel

Start Increasing Profits with the Right Strategy and the Right Talent in Your Business

There is no goal your organization can't achieve with the right plan and the right people. Learn how to stop selling vanilla ice cream and **build the team** to **achieve your dream.**®

- Read along as this book follows a company through a strategy and talent planning process, helping you understanding how to implement it into your organization.

- You will learn how to develop a 3-year vision for your organization, and a 3-year talent plan to achieve it.

- Define "Why" a customer is going to choose you versus a competitor.

- Over 95% of companies who complete this process with advisors from Stop The Vanilla experience an increase in sales and profitability in their **FIRST YEAR**.

- The combination of simultaneously improving on strategy and talent creates individual, team, and organizational performance breakthroughs.

"Without strategy your talent is not focused, without talent your strategy is not executed"

—Steve Van Remortel

Achieving your business, career, and life goals STARTS HERE!

Stop the Vanilla helps leaders achieve the vision for their business, career, and life with the **right strategy** and the **right talent**.

1. Strategy and Talent Consulting Services

Strategy Development

- Strategic planning
- 3-year vision
- Department planning
- Differentiation development—why a customer chooses you
- Target market identification
- Dashboard/measurements
- Plan execution program
- Career and life planning

Talent Development

- Behavioral science assessments
- 3-year talent plan/org structure
- Talent assessment
- Hiring/interviewing process
- Team development
- Leadership development
- Talent engagement/retention
- Succession planning
- Conflict resolution

2. Keynote/Workshop Offerings

Workshop Options

1. How to Develop a 3-Year Vision and 3-Year Talent Plan to Achieve It
2. Team Development Process—Build The Team to Achieve Your Dream®
3. Hire the Right Person the First Time

Keynote Options

1. Stop Selling Vanilla Ice Cream
2. Stop the Vanilla in Your Career and Life

Contact us to set up a **free 15-minute meeting** *to discuss how the right strategy and the right talent could help you achieve the vision for your business, career, and life.*

Info@StoptheVanilla.com • 920-884-8442 • StoptheVanilla.com

About the Author

Steve Van Remortel is an award-winning author, speaker, coach, trainer, consultant, and recognized expert in strategy and talent development. He founded Stop The Vanilla, LLC in 1999 and has since created a library of 100+ strategy and talent planning methodologies. In 2012, Steve authored his first book *Stop Selling Vanilla Ice Cream: Start Increasing Profits with the Right Strategy & Right Talent.* To date, Steve has led over 1,000 strategy and talent planning sessions across hundreds of industries. He has coached thousands of leaders to help them achieve the vision for their business, career and life with the right strategy and the right talent.

Steve is Chief Strategist & Talent Advisor at Stop The Vanilla, LLC. He guides leaders on how to Stop The Vanilla in their business, career, and life through consulting, coaching, live and virtual workshops, and speeches.

Prior to founding Stop The Vanilla, LLC, Steve led a manufacturing company from $4.5 million to $30 million in sales in five years by optimizing the strategy and talent of the organization. He earned his Master's in Strategic Management after a BA in Marketing and Organizational Communications. Steve is a Certified Professional Behavioral Analyst (CPBA) in four behavioral sciences.

Steve and his wife Lisa raised their four children in Green Bay, WI, where he was named Businessperson of the Year. And for the record, his favorite ice cream flavor is Chocolate Chip Cookie Dough. Start a conversation with Steve at either of the following:

 stopthevanilla

 stevevanremortel